Managing Political Conflict

Dennis Pirages
University of Maryland

PRAEGER PUBLISHERS   New York

301.59
P667m

Published in the United States of America in 1976
by Praeger Publishers, Inc.
111 Fourth Avenue, New York, N.Y. 10003

© 1976 by Praeger Publishers, Inc.
All rights reserved

Library of Congress Cataloging in Publication Data

Pirages, Dennis.
  Managing political conflict.

  Bibliography: p. 141
  Includes index.   85-4285
  1. Political sociology. 2. Social conflict.
3. Comparative government. I. Title.
JA76.P55   301.5'92   78-189921
ISBN 0-275-19730-1
ISBN 0-275-84760-8 pbk.

Printed in the United States of America

SERIES EDITOR'S INTRODUCTION

This book is one volume in the Basic Concepts in Political Science series. In one sense, the purpose of these books is to introduce introductory and intermediate undergraduate students to the field of political science. The core volume, *Studying Politics*, presents an overview of the concepts, approaches, and subject matter of the discipline, together with an introduction to elements of critical thinking about the study of politics. Each of the other volumes in the series focuses on one or two central concepts used to describe major areas of political activity. These concept volumes provide definitions of important terms, summarize basic approaches, and describe what political scientists have discovered about the involvement of human beings in these activities—political socialization, the exercise of power and influence, conflict, policy-making, political leadership, the development of political culture, the formation and activities of political groups. By using various combinations of these relatively short books, instructors can structure, as broadly or as selectively as they wish, an introduction to the study of politics for undergraduate students.

In another sense, the purpose of this series is both less "academic" and more ambitious. For this series proceeds from the premise that what political scientists do *qua* political scientists has relevance well beyond the relatively narrow confines of a scholarly discipline. As political science has labored toward greater precision, rigor, and theoretical maturity, it has developed new ways of organizing and studying information about politics.

If one of the goals of science is to provide understanding of our environment, then scientists and nonscientists alike surely share that concern. If this is the case, then our progress as political scientists should hold the promise of improved understanding for nonscientists as well. In short, what political scientists have learned about how to study politics—especially about the close relationship between *what* we know and *how* we find out—ought to be useful to anyone who wants to understand politics. That belief constitutes the principal motivation for this series of books.

In pursuit of that goal, these books attempt to do four things.

First, they introduce students to the language and approaches of political science—not merely as elements of a scholarly discipline, but as useful ways of looking at the world we live in. Second, relatedly, these books raise some basic methodological issues involved in studying politics—not as abstract issues in scholarship but as problems of how we obtain and critically analyze information available to us. Third, the concept-based volumes in this series introduce the student to concrete aspects of political activity through the use of unifying concepts that cut across both traditional subfields of the discipline and formal institutions, or structures, of government. They treat politics as a blend of several types of human behavior. Fourth, the books in the series attempt to overcome the student's natural parochialism—the limitations imposed by his much greater familiarity with the political practices and structures of the society in which he lives—by providing frequent examples of political activity from a variety of cultural settings. In short, the series seeks to be both systematic and concrete. It is designed to provide useful perspectives on an exciting area of human activity, and to present these perspectives in a way that is meaningful for students who are beginning their formal study of the subject.

The task is ambitious, and the accomplishment doubtless will be less than perfect. But the effort seems worthwhile, if we hope to establish the relevance of the discipline of political science not only to theory-building in social science but also to sound, reliable understanding of politics on the part of concerned citizens.

WILLIAM A. WELSH

CONTENTS

Series Editor's Introduction   v

1. **The Origins of Political Conflict**   1

   Biological and Psychological Perspectives on Conflict   1
   Social Organization and Political Conflict   5
   The Group Basis of Conflict   9
   Politics as Conflict   13
   Conflict and Authority   17

2. **Maintaining Political Control**   21

   Elites and Masses   21
   Managing Political Conflict—The Rulers   32
   Creating Citizen Commitment   36
   Industrialization, Stability, Democracy   40

3. **Political Conflict in Developing Countries**   47

   Historical Patterns of Industrialization and Conflict   50
   Authority and Conflict in Developing Countries   56
   Development or Decay?   64

4. **Democracy as Conflict Management**   72

   Democratic Competition: Myths and Reality   72
   Loci of Competition   76
   Nondecisions and Stability   81
   Unresolved Tensions in Democracies   84

5. **Conflict Management Under Socialism**   91

   Access and Legitimacy   94
   Managerial Politics   96
   Building Future Consensus   100
   Creating a New Reality   103

Competition in the New Class   106
   The End of Ideology?   110

6. The Future and Political Conflict   115

   Post-Industrial Society—Conflict and Consensus   116
   Rediscovering the Physical Environment   118
   Managing Post-Industrial Complexity   121

7. Cross-National Studies of Conflict: Concepts and Methods   124

   Refining Concepts   129
   Methodological Questions   132
   Some Conclusions   137

Selected Bibliography   141
Index   145

MANAGING POLITICAL CONFLICT

1
THE ORIGINS OF POLITICAL CONFLICT

Throughout history conflict, violence, bloodshed, and warfare have been enduring characteristics of organized societies. There have been few substantial periods in which there have not been major conflicts among nation-states. A study of twelve European countries and empires spanning twenty-four centuries revealed only four peaceful years for each year that there was violence among them.[1] Repression and violence within nations has also been very common. While the magnitude of overt conflict in some countries, the United States, Great Britain, and other industrial nations, has been slight, many other less industrial countries have been torn with strife. In the 1960s some type of violent civil conflict was experienced by 114 of the world's 121 largest countries and colonies. Since World War II, violent attempts to overthrow governments have been more common than elections in many parts of the world.[2]

Since violent conflict has been so pervasive, academic research has focused most heavily upon its observable and bloody aspects at the expense of substantial analyses of more subtle manifestations. However, violence and bloodshed represent only the extremes of conflict, the tip of an iceberg. Much broader and more interesting is inquiry into less visible forms of conflict and the reasons that overt violence only periodically breaks out in societies where potential for it remains very high. Breaking with this tradition of research on overt violence this book not only considers *why men rebel*, but also examines equally important questions about *why men don't rebel most of the time*.

BIOLOGICAL AND PSYCHOLOGICAL PERSPECTIVES ON CONFLICT

While it may seem unflattering to picture people prior to and within highly organized industrial societies as quarrelsome apes, it is unfortunately true that peaceful settlement of disputes has never been an especially noticeable feature of *Homo sapiens'* evolutionary heritage. Speculations about the human condition in a political "state of nature," which theoretically existed prior to the advent of social and political organization, vary greatly from those portraying the lot of "anarchic man" as blissful paradise to those taking a much dimmer view of primitive living conditions. Many political philosophers have assumed human nature to be basically good and noncombative. It has often been their contention that human beings are corrupted by their social institutions. On the other hand, another school of thought has assumed that human behavior is conditioned by evolution and therefore is as pugnacious as that of other species. Perhaps Thomas Hobbes came close to describing empirical reality when he wrote that without political life and social organization the lot of human beings is to live in *fear* of other persons. In Hobbes' state of nature the "life of man [is] solitary, poor, nasty, brutish, and short."[3]

Not all conflict, aggression, or violence is most profitably studied in political settings, and only a small portion of the studies of such phenomena has been carried out by political scientists. In fact, many theoretical perspectives on conflict and conflict management have originated in biology and psychology and political scientists have borrowed heavily from this literature. Biologists, ecologists, and ethologists have profitably studied conflict among animals. One of the most important concepts linked to animal aggression and, by inference, to aggression among human beings is *territoriality*. Konrad Lorenz has argued that conflict within a species is essential for species survival. Conflict insures that the strongest survive and that they control and protect enough territory to meet nutritional needs. Without territory-based conflict animals would crowd together and exhaust available food supplies in any geographic area. Conflict and aggression, therefore, lead to a sensible distribution of animals over available space and are functional for species survival.[4]

Other observations indicate that, unlike among human beings, fighting within an animal species rarely results in the death of losers. Lorenz has claimed that many animals with sharp beaks and claws could wipe out competition with a single blow, but that inhibitory mechanisms that keep various species from extinguishing themselves have evolved through natural selection. Human beings, however, seem to lack this mechanism. Lorenz claims that this has occurred because human beings evolved without the natural equipment for quick killing and there has been ample opportunity for a loser to "give up" or go through the ritual of pleading for mercy. But modern technology has given humanity the wherewithal to kill large numbers at a great distance. Lack of inhibitory mechanisms could well prove fatal to the human race in an era in which major powers face each other with nuclear-tipped rockets prepared for launching at a moment's notice.[5]

Others have enshrined control of space as an "imperative" and have suggested that this imperative is at the base of human aggression.[6] The evidence for such claims is not compelling, especially since most of it is based upon analogies to lower animals. B. O. Roos has contended that territorial behavior in animals is instinctive, while in human beings it is optional.[7] Certainly human beings exhibit types of territorial behavior ranging from claims to a favorite easy chair to protection of "turf" claimed by neighborhood gangs. But there is little evidence that this type of human territorial behavior is rooted in survival imperatives or natural selection.

Crowding is another concept for which an analogy has been made between lower animals and human beings. The classic animal study in this area was carried out by J. B. Calhoun.[8] He constructed pens into which he put a sexually balanced number of white rats. Over time the rats in each pen multiplied and eventually the density of rats approached a condition defined as "stressful." The number of rats was kept at this stressful level for several generations while Calhoun recorded the behavioral results of crowding. He coined the term "behavioral sink" to describe what he observed to take place. Various abnormalities developed. Normal patterns of nest-building and reproduction were completely destroyed. Some males became aggressive and gathered groups of females into harems. Many males engaged in cannibalism. It was clear that among rats crowding led to the disintegration of normal behavior patterns, to various forms of aggression, and to disruption of reproductive behavior.

Making a link between the results of crowding among animals and human behavior under similar conditions is very difficult, although aggregate data analysis has shown a very high correlation between population density and types of crime and violence.[9] Urban dwellers are much more likely to be involved in robberies, rapes, and various forms of delinquency than are their rural counterparts. Furthermore, mental illness in the inner city has been found to be much more frequent and of a different nature than that which is found in less crowded areas.[10] However, the dynamics underlying the correlation of crowding and crime have yet to be adequately explained given the paucity of data and observations of individuals. Human reactions to crowding are subjective and are conditioned by learned expectations. Conditions that seem crowded to the average American or Western European might not seem at all unusual to a resident of Calcutta.

Psychology and psychiatry have also contributed a number of different perspectives to the study of conflict. Sigmund Freud and his disciples have attributed destructive behavior among human beings to a *death instinct* that occasionally becomes dominant and results in violence and then death. An orthodox Freudian might attribute domestic political violence or even wars among nations to this uncontrolled death wish. Erich Fromm has written extensively about mass behavior and the social psychology of violence. According to Fromm, it is not instinct or a death wish that causes people to become alienated and destructive. The roots of such problems lie in the *nature of technological society*. Fromm's technological society is a lonely and emotionless place where human expression is stifled and where supposedly free individuals seek to escape from their loneliness through mass movements or aggression against others. It is only when the socioeconomic conditions that induce aberrant behavior are altered that aggression, exploitation, and manipulation among people will be eliminated.[11]

Much psychological research has been carried out centering on *frustration* as a cause of aggression. An individual becomes frustrated and then aggressive when an event blocks the attainment of something that is very much desired. Frustration and aggression can be induced in laboratory situations and there seems to be ample evidence of such behavior among human beings.[12] Anthony Storr traces the origins of frustration in individuals back to infancy when they were highly dependent upon parents and frustrated in their attempts at independent acts.[13]

Obedience to authority is another psychological variable that Stanley Milgram has indicated possibly results in human violence and conflict.[14] Milgram has used a laboratory situation to test his theories. An individual (the subject) is ordered by an experimenter (the authority) to administer an electric shock to another person (the confederate) as part of an apparent laboratory memory experiment. The experimenter orders the subject to apply increasingly painful shocks to the confederate who, not really being shocked, pretends to be in increasing pain as the voltage is increased. The object of the experiment is to see if the subject will follow the authority's orders and continue to shock a person who is apparently in great pain. At 75 Volts the confederate groans. At 150 Volts the confederate screams "let me out of here." At 270 Volts the confederate lets out agonizing screams. Milgram has found that under different conditions between one-third and two-thirds of all subjects are willing to give the confederate a full 450-Volt shock upon orders from the experimenter.

Milgram enhanced his experiment by varying the "psychological distance" between the subject, who administered the shock, and the confederate. It is significant that willingness to give the full 450-Volt shock increased as remoteness from the person being shocked increased. Not only did Milgram's experiment confirm that people lack Lorenz's inhibitory mechanisms, particularly when it comes to administering pain under orders from an authority, but it also indicated that people are much more likely to commit violence against others if the acts can be committed from a distance. This has important implications in an era of electronic push-button warfare and instantaneous nuclear destruction.

SOCIAL ORGANIZATION AND POLITICAL CONFLICT

Obviously there is a wealth of information from many other disciplines that could be relevant to the construction of a complete theory of sociopolitical conflict. But while questions concerning the origins of aggression among animals and human beings may be intrinsically interesting, they are somewhat peripheral to the questions to be taken up here about rulers and the ruled and the ways in which political conflict develops and is managed in contemporary societies. When human beings come together to live under organized governments there is little reason to assume that predispositions to fear, aggression, and conflict miraculously disappear. Rather, organized government seeks to routinize conflict and to replace it with peaceful competition whenever possible. Life may become less nasty, brutish, and short in organized society because political institutions are established for sublimating and containing overt conflict, but potential for outbursts of violence remains.

Conflict is inherent in organized society and controlling it is a central function of political processes. There are many types of conflict ranging from that which is very overt and visible to that which is more hidden and covert. Rebellions and riots, for example, are very overt while elections and political campaigns represent a covert and managed form of competition, only distant relatives of more bloody types of encounters.

Contemporary social life is full of potential conflict, although it is not always remarked as such, as one person clashes with others for political, social, or economic gain. This competition among individuals is mirrored on a larger scale in organized competition among corporations, interest groups, political parties, etc. The so-called political arena operates at the center of a carefully regulated struggle within a shifting, but generally agreed upon, set of rules substituting competition for conflict. Violence and bloodshed occur when established social and political mechanisms for containing conflict break down and when one powerful group or another decides that it is no longer worth it to play by these accepted rules. This happens relatively infrequently in industrialized countries and somewhat more frequently in countries where consensus on norms and values is lacking.

Mack and Snyder have made a very useful distinction between competition and conflict.[15] *Competition* involves striving for scarce resources according to sets of rules governing the tactics to be used by competitors. Total destruction of the opposition is not considered to be competition. *Conflict* occurs when competitors disregard rules or when they seek to destroy each other in their quest for scarce resources. A clear distinction between competition and conflict cannot easily be made in the real world. Just as competitors in football or basketball sometimes cheat, political competitors "more or less" follow rules unless they can find ways to effectively circumvent them. One of the tacitly understood rules of the political game is that changing or violating these rules is acceptable as long as violators don't get caught and are willing to pay penalties if they do. Thus, the political competition-conflict relationship is best visualized as a continuum ranging from competitive-nonviolent–nondestructive behavior in conformity with rules at one extreme to conflict-violent–destructive behavior in violation of established norms at the other, with much of the intervening behavior being neither clearly competition nor clearly conflict.

Political competition and conflict in organized society arise over "position scarcity" and "resource scarcity" within an organized structure of rewards.[16] Position scarcity occurs because no two people can occupy the same position in the reward structure at the same time. Nor can one individual occupy two different positions simultaneously. Only a small number of people can occupy positions of great power, privilege, and prestige. Since many people seek them, and since only a few can fill such a limited number of valued positions, conflict frequently develops over them.

Resource scarcity stems both from basic human needs as well as from unlimited human wants in the face of limited physical and social environments. Basic human needs are physiologically determined while wants are socially determined. Particularly in industrial societies socialization processes encourage striving for possession of a limitless amount of goods. Things that are wanted may be tangible (a new automobile) or they may be more socially or psychologically important (various kinds of medals and decorations). The value of objects is determined by the culture or "social paradigm" within which people are socialized, and their wants thus determined. In industrial societies an important man is usually known by the number of material possessions that he has. In less industrial societies an important man may be known by his age, wisdom, or possession of symbolic awards. Among certain tribes of Indians in the American Northwest, an individual exhibited his importance by throwing a "potlatch," a ceremony in which prestige was enhanced by the wealth consumed or destroyed by participants. Whatever their nature and use, the essence of valued resources is that there is never enough to go around and therefore individuals struggle for what there is. Should satiation occur through abundance, other scarce resources would undoubtedly soon become more highly valued.

Since the roots of much conflict are found in scarcity of valued material rewards, a substantial portion of conflict could be said to be economic in origin. In very poor countries conflict of economic origin takes place over shortages of the materials necessary to meet basic needs for food, clothing, and shelter. At present, as well as in the past, supplies of basic commodities are relatively limited and economic conflict is still inevitable in most political systems. The survival of one person has often directly cost the life of another. In contemporary India, for example, the press of hundreds of millions of people against a meager food supply creates conditions that frequently lead to violent incidents, especially among those who are strong enough to fight for food.

While many industrialized nations possess greater material abundance, such economic conflict within them does not disappear. In industrializing countries conflict based on economics actually increases for a number of reasons. Large gaps between the rich and the poor, which are accepted in traditional societies, suddenly become visible irritants in modernizing nations. These gaps are less tolerable in the face of a revolution of rising expectations, a general increase in wants brought on by industrialization and the accompanying rapid growth of mass media.

It is to be expected that economic conflict, much of which is eventually politicized, often takes the form of conflict among economic classes over distribution of rewards. Karl Marx was the foremost proponent of a class view of history. He saw a world in which a shrinking number of wealthy industrialists controlled the means of industrial production (investment capital, factories, natural resources, etc.) and squeezed ever more labor from a helpless working class (the proletariat). Marx saw this conflict as being essential to the transformation of capitalist industrial society, with its class-based conflict and inequities, into a society that would be more egalitarian, one in which conflict would disappear and in which each person would contribute according to his abilities and receive according to his needs. Needless to say, no society has yet approached the Marxist ideal, although present-day socialist economies have made considerable progress in narrowing gaps between the rich and the poor and in providing basic services to all citizens.[17] Capitalist countries have narrowed income gaps very slowly, and recently there have been indications that movement toward egalitarian capitalist societies may have come to a halt.[18] The evening of income distributions has not been due to any revolt from the proletariat, which Marx thought would rise up to seize the means of production. Rather, it has often been due to increasingly effective organization of competition through labor unions and to the ideological importance of the working class in those countries where socialist revolutions have taken place.

Since man does not live by bread alone, economic conflict is by no means extinct in those few societies in which material resources are sufficient to guarantee a reasonable standard of living to all. Human beings are material-oriented animals, each person seeming to expect higher levels of living in the future and predicating expectations on what other people are perceived to have. The revolution of rising expectations is not limited to industrializing countries. Under conditions of relative abundance, expectations continue to be shaped by more affluent "reference groups" with which individuals identify. Rising expectations in industrial societies are not based on physical needs for food, clothing, or shelter. Rather they are based on new sets of expectations created by a psychic need to keep up with others. Thus, an individual might be quite content to drive a small automobile until neighbors buy larger ones. This desire to "keep up with the Joneses" may seem to be irrational, but it is a fact of economic life with very important political consequences. These psychological dynamics create resource scarcity even where there is abundance and will be a source of social and political conflict for the foreseeable future, as people continue to create scarce resources even under conditions of relative economic abundance.

Psychologist Abraham Maslow touched on this point when he posited a typology that he called a hierarchy of human needs. According to Maslow, human beings possess a variety of different needs that become "prepotent" under different conditions. The most basic needs for food, clothing, and shelter are always present and monopolize consciousness until they are satisfied. Higher level needs begin to monopolize attention only after lower level needs are met. In Maslow's hierarchy physiological and safety needs are most basic. Once physiological and safety needs are met, needs for love and affection become prepotent, then needs for esteem, and finally needs for self-actualization. Obviously, physiological and safety needs are related to resource scarcity while position scarcity is closely related to needs for love, esteem, and opportunities for self-actualization.[19] As some societies have become more industrialized and more affluent, a much larger portion of the population finds basic physiological needs to be met and turns its psychic attention to those higher in the need hierarchy. Thus, once competition for food and shelter diminishes, more people turn to satisfying psychic needs for love, esteem, and seek opportunities to self-actualize. Psychologically, then, when objective scarcity of material artifacts is not a factor determining competition and conflict, people seek other scarce resources associated with love, esteem, and self-actualization.

THE GROUP BASIS OF CONFLICT

Conflict and competition may originate in resource and position scarcity, but conflict takes place, is magnified, crystallized, and reinforced within organized groups. Most political systems embrace millions of individuals each of whom brings a somewhat different set of aspirations, beliefs, preferences, and psychological needs to politics. Each person is socialized in a slightly different social environment, and therefore people and groups come to the political arena with different sets of expectations and policy preferences. Those factors that make individuals and groups unique are also factors that can lead to sharp divisions.

Human beings have been called "social animals" because of this tendency to form groups. High levels of interaction in groups lead to development of shared norms and preferences.[20] Political processes reconcile the very real differences in perspectives that follow these group lines of cleavage. In relatively homogenous societies or those in which there are many different group memberships that overlap this may well be possible. But in other societies, where positions on policies harden along group lines, stability is highly unlikely.

One of the factors which leads to group identification and hence to differing policy preferences is *race*. One of the easiest ways to define membership in an "in-group" is by physical characteristics such as skin coloring, type of hair, or facial features. In the United States, Great Britain, and South Africa, for example, racial distinctions have most frequently been made between blacks and whites. In these and other nations persons of other colors also have suffered at the hands of either whites or blacks. Race has often been used by dominant majorities to deny racial minorities access to status, prestige, and opportunity and thus as a method of setting rules of competition within which majorities retain a large competitive edge. It is worth noting that until the late 1950s many black citizens of the United States were not even given basic civil rights and were relegated to permanent resource and position inferiority by a white majority.

Conflict also hardens along *ethnic* lines. In situations where obvious physical markings do not separate one group from another, different languages and cultural characteristics often serve as substitutes. Thus, in Canada conflict between French- and English-speaking Canadians has frequently erupted into violence as the French minority has tried to preserve its own cultural identity. In Belgium similar conflict has repeatedly taken place between the Flems and Walloons, each group being dedicated to preserving its language and culture and occasionally to imposing this language and culture on others.

Racial and ethnic differences are often reinforced by geographic factors and *regionalism*. History has left a legacy of serious regional cleavage in almost all nation-states. Before the industrial revolution, the idea of unified nations of tens or hundreds of millions of people was only a dream. Most large political systems were empires consisting of small fiefdoms knit together into larger coalitions. It was simply impossible for rulers to centrally administer a large amount of territory because of transportation and communication difficulties.[21] Thus, small enclaves developed and retained different social and political customs and perspectives, and some of these differences persist today as important political issues. In many countries in the northern hemisphere these regional divisions fall along a north-south axis. Thus, in the United States, France, Italy, Poland, Yugoslavia, Germany, and many other countries the southern portion of each country is less industrially developed and is characterized by different types of sociopolitical attitudes and values. In the Soviet Union and China there are also very significant regional differences, not necessarily of a north-south nature, and much political strife has occurred in stemming secessionist movements.

Numerous other factors are important in group identification and the development of differing social and political perspectives. *Religious strife,* for example, has been responsible for a tremendous amount of bloodshed and a very large number of deaths throughout history. Religious conflict has frequently been politicized through the imposition of state religions and various types of theocracies. *Ideologies,* often closely related to religion, have similarly been responsible for creating conflict and bloodshed as one or another group possessing fervent beliefs has attempted to "convert" others by use of force. Thus, communist movements in numerous countries have been responsible for many ideology-related deaths. Although those who have been socialized in capitalist countries don't often think of capitalism as an ideology, defense of this economic belief system has been at least partially responsible for many deaths.

Historically, perhaps the greatest cause of overt violence among nations has been various aspects of *nationalism.* Nation-states are political units composed of people who identify with each other and feel linked by a common destiny. Karl Deutsch has used the term "covariance" to describe the essence of nationhood. Covariance, or "we" feeling, is related to the idea that the prosperity of the collective (the nation) is linked to the prosperity of the individual. It is individual perception of this common fate that links people together in a nation-state. High levels of communication among individuals are essential to the establishment of nation-states as well as to the development of covariance.[22] Nation-states are to this time the largest organized group characterized by "we" feeling among group members. Humanity has unfortunately not yet overcome nationalist thinking; people do not yet identify themselves as citizens of the world.

Particularly in formerly colonized areas of the world, the boundaries of nations characterized by covariance don't correspond with contemporary state boundaries. Where there is no such nation and state congruence, separatist movements based on regional, tribal, cultural, or religious divisions are common. Such separatist groups are often willing to fight for their own "national" interests and independence from what are considered to be oppressive governments. Frequently lacking sufficient armed strength to break completely with the larger political unit, secessionist movements resort to guerrilla warfare in order to make their retention as part of the state a great liability.

Aggressive nationalism has created much of the violence among nation-states that has dominated world history. Political leaders encourage development of nationalism because it is easier to govern a unified group of people linked by strong nationalistic feelings. These nationalistic feelings occasionally spill over into wars of aggression against other nation-states. The resulting violence represents the ultimate extension of the in-group, out-group cleavages that are characteristic of organized social groups.

All of the above factors—economic and psychological needs, resource and position scarcity, and race, ethnicity, religion, ideology, regionalism, and nationalism—represent potential sources of conflict in different societies at different times. But conflict does not always result from seemingly volatile mixtures. Potential conflict can lie dormant for decades if political leaders optimally use their managerial resources. Racial issues, for example, were a potential source of friction throughout American history, but after the Civil War they lay dormant until racial discrimination and equality of opportunity became issues in the Civil Rights movement of the 1950s and 1960s. Income redistribution has been a potentially serious political issue in many countries, since large differences between the incomes of the rich and the incomes of the poor are nearly universal, but, by itself, consciousness of economic differences has rarely led to political conflict. Religious issues have been a latent source of conflict over the centuries, but they have often been defused by clever political moves such as separation of church and state.

Special conditions do exist under which latent sources of social conflict become politicized. In developing nations, for example, ethnic strife and regionalism are very frequently politicized, but in economically developed countries such issues are normally submerged by economic affluence. In industrial countries, by contrast, there is a very tight link between general economic conditions and political stability, inflation and unemployment often spelling the downfall of governments. The extent to which the political arena is perceived as a place to settle disputes through competition or the extent to which open conflict emerges varies with national experience, which is cumulatively reflected in the development of a unique "political culture" or "dominant political paradigm" in each nation-state.[23] Some of the reasons that latent conflict becomes politicized or overt are dealt with in greater detail below.

Politics as Conflict

Political systems are conditioned by constraints found in both social and physical environments. Political leaders must manage these environments and must be responsive to pressures from them. As outlined above, all societies are characterized by a shortage of valued resources and positions ranging from food and shelter to opportunities for economic advancement and exercise of power. Resource scarcity can be managed by successful manipulation of physical environments. Position scarcity can be managed by successful manipulation of social environments. Political leaders attempt to formulate policies through which optimal manipulation of these environments may take place and conflict can thus be avoided.

There are many different perspectives from which analysis of political conflict management can begin. One alternative stresses politics as a *cooperative undertaking* involving the coordination of a division of labor within society. From this viewpoint political leaders can be depicted as guardians or helmsmen steering the proverbial ship of state through murky waters. Working from this perspective an analyst seeks to find answers to questions such as how nation-states hold together in the face of the many centripetal tendencies found in industrial societies. Thus, sociologist Talcott Parsons and political scientist Gabriel Almond, among others, have studied the "integrative" and "adaptive" functions of social and political systems. "The political system is [seen as] the legitimate, order-maintaining or transforming system in society."[24] The point of departure that stresses the cooperative aspect of politics highlights the differences between living in a state of nature and living in a society with organized management that makes life less nasty, brutish, and short. Politics can be depicted as a gigantic managerial planning operation in which collective goals are decided and a social division of labor in meeting these goals is coordinated.

Cooperation in meeting goals is an important aspect of politics, but it is utopian to expect human beings to consider only collective good or general welfare when participating in politics. Frequently individual appetites overcome any vision of planning and cooperation in the interest of the collective, and a *conflict perspective* on politics is often much more appropriate. Since there are limited quantities of scarce resources and coveted positions, it is too much to expect a majority of citizens to put collective interest ahead of self-interest. Thus, a vast body of political inquiry has focused on various aspects of political conflict, often using power relationships as a definition of political activity. From this conflict perspective, the social contract only represents a modest agreement to mediate and routinize conflict through political processes.

When conflict is taken to be the essence of politics and the exercise of power determines the boundaries of political inquiry, however, almost all human behavior can be defined as political. Hierarchies and the associated use of power are found in all organizations, and various forms of conflict and competition, ranging from riots, rebellions, and political campaigns to collective bargaining, work stoppages, or family quarrels, pervade social life. Clearly, more appropriate boundaries of political inquiry must be carefully drawn.

Although political scientists have attempted to delineate the boundaries of their profession in hundreds of ways, a definition of politics offered by David Easton is useful and inclusive. He has defined politics as the "authoritative allocation of values" for society.[25] The values that are allocated by political processes vary from concrete (tangible) resources and positions to those that are symbolic (intangible). Such things as wages and salaries, housing, income taxes, government largess, or welfare fall into the former category. Presidential medals, hero of socialist labor awards, or other intangible symbolic objects fall into the latter category. Political institutions determine the rules within which individuals compete for or conflict over scarce resources and positions.

An *authoritative allocation* of values implies the occasional use of force to maintain order. Thus, a conflict perspective on political processes with emphasis on maintaining stability has been the dominant one in political science. But this is not to imply that conflict has universally been seen as an unfortunate or pathological condition. Revolutionaries and other advocates of drastic social change recognize that change often takes place only through violence and that stability may be a sign of repression. Lack of competition or conflict over scarce resources and positions might actually be a sign of restricted freedom.

Political leaders seek to minimize conflict, largely by encompassing as many divergent views as possible within the framework of peaceful competition. While minimization of conflict is considered to be a worthy end, this does not imply that the elimination of all forms of conflict is possible or desirable. Diversity and innovation are often spawned by conflict. Far from being utopias, societies in which there is very little overt conflict are likely to be boring places in which to live if not actually dangerous by virtue of being dictatorships or powder kegs of repressed conflict about to explode.

Conflict-management, in contrast with conflict minimization or elimination, is an active process undertaken by all political incumbents in seeking to maintain political stability and themselves in power. One obvious strategy of conflict management is responsiveness to various citizen demands whenever possible. Conflict management also often involves the substitution of more remote issues for those that are in the public eye and that are more dangerous and pressing. Another tactic that has not infrequently been used by ruling political elites is the substitution of conflicts with foreign powers when internal problems become unmanageable. Nations beset by an economic depression, for example, have sometimes engaged other nations on the battlefield in order to distract attention from internal problems and to stimulate economic growth.

E. E. Schattschneider has written extensively about the management and displacement of conflict in American politics. The points that he has made apply to British politics as well. According to Schattschneider there are any number of possible conflicts that could attract public attention at any one time. Since only a small number of potential conflicts can become significant without overburdening decision-making processes, political parties and organizations carefully choose the issues that they wish to emphasize. Political processes are devoted to the domination and subordination of these many potential conflicts. All political leaders, all political parties, and all political and quasi-political organizations are involved in the narrowing of political issues and conflicts to a workable number as well as in the substitution of more manageable for less manageable lines of cleavage.[26]

Although conflict and competition are inherent in any distribution of valued resources and positions, many scholars have written extensively of the *virtues* of social conflict. Sociologist Lewis Coser, for example, has emphasized the unifying role that conflict plays in coalition formation, maintaining balances of power, and creating greater understanding of potential enemies.[27] Within political systems conflict is essential to the organization and preservation of political coalitions. In relations among nations conflict is often critical in checking the ambitions of powerful nations and thus in preserving long-term stability and a balance of power. Conflict also generates some respect for and certainly understanding of an enemy. The United States and Great Britain are now strongly allied politically and economically with Germany and Japan, two nations that the Allies fought during World War II.

Coser has also elaborated Georg Simmel's contention that absence of conflict in relationships is not necessarily an index of harmony and stability.[28] Parties to a relationship feel free to express hostilities only within what they perceive to be fairly stable situations. Where relationships are perceived to be fragile the parties involved may very well "walk on eggs" to preserve them. Politically this means that the president of the United States or the British prime minister is not likely to make a major address voicing criticism of the Soviet Union or China without expecting serious consequences. By the same token, less thought would be given to voicing criticism of an ally, such as Norway or the Netherlands, if it were deemed necessary, because the long history of stability in relations with these countries indicates mild and predictable reactions. Thus, absence of overt hostility in interchanges among leaders of large nations does not necessarily imply a condition of peace and stability.

An apparent lack of measurable conflict within political systems is also often taken as a sign of domestic political health while in reality it could represent a truce between warring factions, a sort of "calm before the storm." It could also result from a heavy investment in repressive force. Many of the world's most disagreeable dictators have governed apparently stable societies, often until sudden revolutions occurred. The essential point is that it is often necessary to look beyond measurable indicators of violence and conflict in order to assess appropriately the potential for future political violence or instability, something to keep in mind when reading cross-national studies of conflict.

Conflict and Authority

Politics is called the authoritative allocation of values because those who make major decisions have power to enforce them. Ruling political elites derive much of their *authority,* and thus their ability to manage conflict successfully, from the fact that their acts are approved by the citizens in whose name they rule. "Authority is the quality inherent in a legitimate political organization or process which predisposes individuals to conform to its rules."[29] When the actions taken and allocations made by political elites correspond to citizen demands and expectations authority is enhanced. Obviously the larger the amount of resources or number of positions available for distribution the more likely will authority be maintained. But it is impossible to satisfy all of the people all of the time. Thus, a monopoly of the use of force is another important aspect of political authority. While authority often grows from democratic elections of political officials and approval of their actions, it also frequently comes from the barrels of automatic weapons.

Authority is closely tied to *legitimacy.* Gilison has pointed out that "a legitimate political organization, role, or process is defined as one which people feel ought to exist because it conforms, in whole or in part, to principles which are considered morally good." He goes on to describe five ways in which political regimes acquire legitimacy:

1. They are reasonably efficient in performing economic and other functions.
2. They retain control of important components of the political system over time.
3. They generally conform to prevailing social values.
4. They use educational systems and mass media to inculcate supportive values.
5. They are sufficiently responsive to the needs of subjects.[30]

Political regimes strive for legitimacy because affective (emotional) bonds between citizens and government are much more efficient in maintaining authority over time than are guns and tanks.

Gaining a complete understanding of who makes an authoritative allocation of values in society and discovering the countless points at which political conflict may occur is a very complex task. First, the political elites who determine value allocations must be identified. Obviously those holding elective or appointive public office, the "ruling political elites," are critical, but in all societies many others are an important part of the political process by virtue of their influence over allocations and therefore belong to the "ruling elite." Economic and social leaders influence the allocation of values through decisions made within their own spheres of competence as well as through social and economic pressures that they may bring to bear on formal decision-making. In the United States, as in many other capitalist countries, financial resources are very important in determining allocations. Persons possessing a great deal of economic power, such as the chairman of the board of General Motors or of United States Steel, make private decisions that greatly influence the social allocation of values and their decisions are every bit as important as those of elected political leaders. As an example, when former Secretary of Defense Robert McNamara was being recruited by the Kennedy administration to become a member of the ruling political elite, he was first offered the position of secretary of the treasury which, he was told, would permit him to set the country's interest rates. He replied, "Hell, I do more at Ford [of which he was president] about setting the interests than the secretary of the treasury."[31]

Individuals who combine within the framework of large organizations, such as trade unions or political parties, can do much more to influence allocations than those who remain isolated. Political competition and conflict, therefore, do not take place within a tidy framework of well-understood allocation rules and among equals; rather, in this competition some are more equal than others in influencing the allocation of values.

Easton's model of politics stresses the importance for political leaders to be judicious and intelligent in allocating scarce resources and positions. When citizen demands *appear* to be met by political leaders, political authority and legitimacy increase. When these demands are not perceived to be met, however, citizen support is withdrawn. Political conflict management involves strategies aimed at both the management of demands and the optimal use of resources and positions to build citizen support.

REFERENCES

Note to the Reader: An attempt has been made to reduce redundancy in the notes that follow. This means that page numbers have been omitted when an entire article or book chapter is cited. In addition, months and years have been substituted for volumes and numbers of journals in the interest of simplicity. The principle that has guided this venture is one of saving paper and ink while still permitting the reader to quickly locate any desired reference.

1. P. Sorokin, *Social and Cultural Dynamics*. Volume III: *Fluctuations of Social Relationships, War, and Revolutions*. New York: American Book Company, 1937. P. Sorokin's estimates are more recently found in R. Prosterman, *Surviving to 3000: An Introduction to the Study of Lethal Conflict*. Belmont, Calif.: Duxbury Press, 1972, p. 37.
2. T. Gurr, *Why Men Rebel*. Princeton: Princeton University Press, 1970, p. 3.
3. T. Hobbes, *Leviathan*. New York: Bobbs-Merrill, 1958, ch. 13.
4. K. Lorenz, *On Aggression*. New York: Harcourt, Brace and World, 1966, pp. 30ff.
5. Lorenz, *On Aggression*, p. 240ff.
6. R. Ardrey, *The Territorial Imperative*. New York: Atheneum, 1966.
7. B. O. Roos, "Jurisdiction: An Ecological Concept," *Human Relations* 21 (1968).
8. J. Calhoun, "Population Density and Social Pathology," *Scientific American* (February 1962).
9. W. Ittelson et al., *An Introduction to Environmental Psychology*. New York: Holt, Rinehart & Winston, 1974, pp. 254–58.
10. A. Hollingshead and F. Redlick, *Social Class and Mental Illness*. New York: Wiley, 1958; and R. Faris and H. Dunham, *Mental Disorders in Urban Areas*. Chicago: University of Chicago Press, 1939.
11. E. Fromm, *The Sane Society*. New York: Holt, Rinehart & Winston, 1955; and E. Fromm, *The Revolution of Hope: Toward a Humanized Technology*. New York: Harper and Row, 1968.
12. J. Dollard, *Frustration and Aggression*. New Haven: Yale University Press, 1939; and L. Berkowitz, *Aggression: A Social Psychological Analysis*. New York: McGraw-Hill, 1962.
13. A. Storr, *Human Aggression*. New York: Atheneum, 1968, ch. 5.

14. S. Milgram, "Behavioral Study of Obedience," *The Journal of Abnormal and Social Psychology* 4 (1963).
15. R. Mack and R. Snyder, "The Analysis of Social Conflict—Toward an Overview and Synthesis," *The Journal of Conflict Resolution* (June 1957): 217.
16. Mack and Snyder, "The Analysis of Social Conflict—Toward an Overview and Synthesis," p. 218.
17. The problem of computing income differences in socialist societies is a difficult one. See P. Wiles and S. Markowski, "Income Distribution under Communism and Capitalism: Some Facts about Poland, the United Kingdom, the U.S.A. and the U.S.S.R.," *Soviet Studies* (January and April 1971).
18. S. Rose, "The Truth about Income Inequality in the U.S." *Fortune* (December 1972).
19. A. Maslow, "A Theory of Human Motivation," in P. Harriman, ed., *Twentieth Century Psychology*. New York: The Philosophical Library, 1946.
20. K. Deutsch discusses political aspects of communication, interaction, and development of common norms in detail in "Communication Theory and Political Integration," in K. Deutsch et al., *The Integration of Political Communities*. Philadelphia: Lippincott, 1964.
21. See K. Deutsch, *Nationalism and Social Communication: An Inquiry into the Foundations of Nationality*. Cambridge: M.I.T. Press, 1953, ch. 3.
22. Deutsch, *Nationalism and Social Communication*, ch. 4.
23. S. Verba, "Comparative Political Culture," in L. Pye and S. Verba, eds., *Political Culture and Political Development*. Princeton: Princeton University Press, 1965. See also D. Pirages and P. Ehrlich, *Ark II: Social Response to Environmental Imperatives*. San Francisco: W. H. Freeman, 1974, ch. 2, for a more detailed explanation of the role dominant paradigms play in orienting social life.
24. G. Almond and J. Coleman, eds., *The Politics of Developing Areas*. Princeton: Princeton University Press, 1960, p. 7.
25. D. Easton, *The Political System*. New York: Knopf, 1953.
26. E. Schattschneider, *The Semi-Sovereign People: A Realist's View of Democracy*. New York: Holt, Rinehart & Winston, 1960, ch. 4.
27. L. Coser, *The Functions of Social Conflict*. Glencoe, Ill.: Free Press, 1956, pp. 121–28, 133–37, 139–49.
28. Coser, *The Functions of Social Conflict*, pp. 81–85.
29. J. Gilison, *British and Soviet Politics: Legitimacy and Convergence*. Baltimore: The Johns Hopkins University Press, 1972, p. 7.
30. Gilison, *British and Soviet Politics*, p. 9.
31. Quoted in D. Halberstam, *The Best and the Brightest*. New York: Random House, 1972, p. 223.

2
MAINTAINING POLITICAL CONTROL

ELITES AND MASSES

In his book *Political Parties* Roberto Michels penned the short, classic statement "to say organization is to say oligarchy."[1] His so-called iron law of oligarchy is accepted as a statement of political fact. Although it is actually a statement of very high probability, rather than an iron law, it is true that there are very few, if any, large organizations that are not run by a tightly knit group of self-perpetuating elites. Any organization that wishes to persist and successfully meet its goals, whatever these goals may be, must have a small oligarchy capable of making decisions for the collective membership or it is likely to be eliminated by competitors. An oligarchy concentrates decisional power in a few hands, gives an organization flexibility, and permits rapidity in responding to external challenges. This holds true for labor unions and corporations, as well as national political systems. The larger an organization, the more heterogenous its membership, the more serious competitive threats to its existence, the greater the need for strong centralized leadership capable of forging policies that enable the organization to persist and meet its stated goals.

National political systems are seldom thought of as organizations, although they clearly qualify as such. Nations are run by oligarchies, just as are other organizations, and the societies in which these political systems exist have collective goals as well as an intricate division of labor aimed at meeting these goals. A country's goals may be many and more varied than those of smaller organizations. They range from very universal economic goals, such as full employment or economic development, to goals of conquest and dominance.

The composition, size, and goal orientations of ruling oligarchies vary from country to country. Historically, many smaller primitive societies were not able to afford the luxury of a large ruling class. Supporting a sizable oligarchy requires economic surplus and at least a rudimentary division of labor. Many hunting and gathering societies never reached this level of complexity. In such small societies a "head man" or "elder" did all the authoritative allocating of values that took place. This was possible because the collective problems that needed to be solved were not technically complex. But as first an agricultural and then an industrial revolution expanded the size and complexity of societies and increased economic productivity, the size and jurisdiction of ruling oligarchies increased accordingly.

Not only has the size of oligarchies increased, along with an increasingly complex division of labor and economic surplus, but the rules for selection to them have also changed. Throughout most of recorded history, selection to ruling oligarchies has taken place by means of *ascription* rather than *achievement*.[2] Selection by ascription is based on factors not under an individual's control; characteristics with which one is born. Thus, family lineage, order of birth, and sex are ascriptive characteristics that have frequently determined the composition of ruling oligarchies. Mass democracy, featuring election of ruling political elites by secret ballot, ostensibly on the basis of achievement and competence, is a fairly recent political innovation and represents a marked departure from traditional methods.

Elected or selected members of political oligarchies are referred to as *ruling political elites* in contrast with the more general term ruling elites, which refers to all those who are influential in the allocation of values, whether formally elected, self-appointed, or otherwise found in a position of influence. In contemporary political systems methods of recruiting ruling political elites and their relationship with the ruled masses vary. The most important differentiating variable would seem to be *insulation from citizen pressure*. Insulation is closely related to the style in which an oligarchy rules. In democracies the degree of insulation of ruling political elites from mass pressures is usually relatively small while under various types of authoritarian regimes it is rather great. There are many exceptions to this general rule, however. In some democracies in which there are very few unresolved social conflicts and in which economic productivity is increasing, ruling elites usually accumulate a balance of citizen good will permitting them a great deal of latitude in framing collective policies. In more authoritarian societies, by contrast, unresolved social conflicts and economic difficulties sometimes threaten political stability, and even dictators must pay careful attention to citizen demands under these conditions.

Arthur Banks and Robert Gregg have studied empirically the ways in which political systems differ and have found that *insulation of ruling political elites* makes the most significant difference. The authors used a complicated factor analysis technique to analyze cross-national data in order to identify a cluster of sociopolitical variables that are empirically related to elite insulation. They labeled this cluster "access" to decision-making. Access is defined by dichotomies such as hierarchical as opposed to competitive bargaining processes, consolidated as opposed to distributed authority and force, executive and single-party politics as opposed to legislative and group politics, and totalitarian restrictions on politics as opposed to institutionalized openness of political channels. Much can be predicted about the characteristics of a society and political system once the degree of citizen access to political decision-making is known. This includes such things as the number of competitive political parties, the level of economic development, the existence of serious social cleavages, the likelihood of military intervention in political affairs, the nature of the legislative branch, the degree press freedom, etc.[3]

In democracies citizens by definition have a great deal of access to politicians and the political arena. One route is through periodic election of ruling political elites and, once they are elected, lobbying and otherwise influencing them. A second is more direct and is related to the freedom of all citizens to run for office. In reality, however, ruling political elites are usually well insulated from citizen pressures, even in democracies, and direct access to office by running in elections is limited by finances to a fairly small segment of the population. In the United States the wealthiest twenty percent of the population contributes about ninety percent of all ruling political elites on the national level and this same wealthy twenty percent has a much greater opportunity to influence legislation.[4] Different people have different chances of obtaining access to the political arena and it helps to be born into the right family, to be a member of the upper classes, to attend the right schools, and to internalize the "proper" social and political attitudes.

In authoritarian countries the rules by which one gains access to decision-making are very stringent and political power rests in the hands of smaller numbers. In the Soviet Union, for example, real decisional power is concentrated in the Politbureau of the

Communist Party of the Soviet Union, which has about twenty members, and the Party Secretariat, which is directed by about ten key members. There is a set of rules by which a person gains admission to this inner sanctum and it includes such things as a working-class background, ideological purity as evidenced by attendance at higher party schools, and years of careful maneuvering within the Communist Party apparatus.

Insulation of ruling political elites from mass pressures in most industrial democracies is an established fact. There are both good and bad consequences of this insulation depending upon perspective. One school of political thought has decried the existence of a small monied oligarchy in American politics and has argued that ruling elites in general and ruling political elites in particular should be much more accountable to the masses.[5] Even within this school, however, there have been differences of opinion over the role that should be played by the common man in politics. Some would simply replace the present monied elite with one based on education, others would expand the ruling oligarchy slightly while avoiding a commitment to mass politics, and still others argue very strongly for mass participation in political decision-making.[6] Another school of political thought, the elitist school with historical roots in the work of Plato, has argued strongly for maintaining elite insulation from mass pressures as the only way to avoid government by the uninformed and the tyranny that would certainly follow.[7] It is clear, for example, that mass political participation in less developed countries often leads to political instability. In these political systems elite insulation is required if goals of economic development are to be met. Where expectations run high and the positions and resources available to ruling political elites for allocation are few, insulation of ruling elites from mass pressures is essential to the maintenance of political stability.

Another important dimension of difference among the world's political systems is the *scope* and *pervasiveness* of ruling political elite control. Scope refers to the sectors of social and economic activity within which ruling political elites are able to effectively assert their authority. Pervasiveness, on the other hand, refers to the depth or substance of actions which can be taken by ruling political elites within the areas that they control.

Some countries have a tradition of "limited government"; which is to say that the scope within which government is able to exert its authority is very limited. The United States has such a tradition. Ruling political elites would not think of infringing upon many social, economic, and political freedoms. There is no state religion in the United States. Married couples are not told how many children to have. The educational system is decentralized and curricula remain largely in the hands of state and local officials. Government ownership of businesses or control of economic activity is anathema and even limited wage and price controls, designed to combat inflation, have been scorned. No one expects and most would not permit the congress or the president to restrict the right to peacefully assemble, the right to press freedoms, or the right to freedom of inquiry.

In other countries, however, the scope of government authority is much greater. In the Soviet Union ruling political elites assume responsibility for regulating all types of activity ranging from religious practices to the socialist economy. According to Soviet doctrine regulation of socioeconomic activity is essential in moving from a socialist society (one in which workers own the means of production through their government and in which there are no classes based on property ownership) to a communist society (a classless society within which everyone contributes according to ability and receives according to needs).

Pervasiveness in political management is normally closely related to scope of political control, but this does not have to be the case. Pervasiveness refers to the freedom with which ruling political elites can take substantive, in-depth actions in any of the areas that fall within their scope of control. Thus, in communist China or the Soviet Union political leaders have both wide scope of control and great pervasiveness in any particular area. In the United States, Canada, or Australia, however, both the scope and pervasiveness of ruling political elite control is very restricted. Not only do political leaders keep hands off so-called free economies in these countries, but there is much citizen resistance to government control in all sectors of society. There are some nations in which great scope of ruling political elite control is combined with very little pervasiveness and others in which great pervasiveness in some areas is combined with very little scope. Examples of the former are Yugoslavia or Poland, both countries within which ruling political elites constitutionally have extensive power to control political, social, economic, and cultural affairs, but countries in which great depth or pervasiveness of government control is not tolerated. Many dictatorships, such as pre-1975 Spain, would fall into the latter category where pervasiveness of dictatorial actions may be very great in some areas but where many spheres of activity, especially economic activity, remain by custom in private hands.

Differences in the scope and pervasiveness of elite control are closely related to political conflict and conflict management. In so-called totalitarian political systems, those in which there is very great scope of central control and pervasive government presence in social, economic, and cultural affairs, responsibility for ethnic, racial, and class conflict, economic failures, or even religious problems is frequently attributed to ruling political elites. In countries in which control is more "total," conflict of all types is much more quickly politicized. In those countries in which the scope and pervasiveness of political control is restricted, social or economic conflicts do not necessarily become politicized as ruling political elites are often not perceived as being responsible for them. Thus, throughout United States and British history there have been extended periods of social strife that have not been reflected in extreme dissatisfaction with political leaders. Nationwide strikes have occasionally crippled both economies, but political leaders have not been overthrown because of them, partly because this type of competition or conflict has not been thought of as the responsibility of ruling political elites. In communist countries, where political control is more pervasive, if there is no bread on grocery store shelves the ruling communist parties are held responsible by the public.

A third way in which political systems differ is *elite composition and the extent to which ruling political elites are representative* of the whole society. In more traditional political systems ruling political elites are selected by ascription and drawn from an extremely narrow section of the population. The basis for selection is most frequently family background; members of certain families are expected to assume leadership positions upon the death of their parents. Leaders rarely retire before death.

In modernizing societies ruling political elites are likely to be strongmen, dictators, or military figures. Problems of social change and conflict involved in making a transition from a traditional society to a more secular and industrial one create conflicts between older generations, living by one set of customs and beliefs, and younger generations that have embraced a new way of life.

Strong leadership is required to preserve stability in transitional societies moving toward modernization goals.

Industrialization creates a more complex society requiring the managerial talents of a highly educated and specialized ruling political elite. Specialized expertise is reflected either in the election of qualified individuals or through the selection of educated advisory staffs. Achievement criteria become more important as candidates for office must at least pretend to possess the expertise required to deal with a host of socioeconomic problems. In the Soviet Union the need for such specialists has resulted in tensions between old-line "politicians" and younger "technocrats." In the United States such cleavage has not been quite so obvious, although the disappearance of old "ward bosses" and their replacement by younger reformers seems to be part of a similar process.

Under no conditions do the socioeconomic backgrounds of ruling political elites resemble that of a society as a whole. It has been argued that political elites frequently come from "socially marginal" segments of society and that demographic trends within ruling political elites often run counter to demographic trends for the population as a whole. Furthermore, demographic attributes such as nationality, religious orientation, or density of population in area of birth have been found to be very important predictors of mass attitudes, but these variables reveal very little as predictors of attitudes among ruling political elites. Thus, it is not at all unlikely to find Roman Catholic leaders coming from Protestant areas of a country or Protestant leaders coming from Roman Catholic areas. It is also not unusual to find ruling political elites making decisions that go against the values of the populace living in their place of birth.[8]

It is important to keep in mind that, whereas most of the emphasis to this point has been on ruling *political* elites, there are other ruling elites in religion, business, the military, etc. who also play an important role in affecting an authoritative allocation of values. The barrier between this social, economic, military, and cultural elite and the ruling political elite is permeable. Business and military leaders, for example, frequently move into the political arena and political leaders often retire to key business positions when they suffer political defeats. There are many types of elites responsible for making decisions that affect the lives of all citizens and they are both within and outside of the formal political arena.

MAINTAINING POLITICAL STABILITY—THE RULED

Given the rather sharp divisions between the social origins and life styles of ruling political elites and ruled masses in almost all political systems, it is difficult to understand how political stability can be maintained over time. Ruling political elites are always badly outnumbered by those whom they rule, and it would appear that they might frequently be in danger of being forcibly removed from office by angry and envious mobs. Harry Eckstein has noted that there are two parties to internal warfare, the insurgents and the incumbents, and that successful revolutionary movements can be explained either by the successes of the rebels or the failures of incumbents.[9] Similarly, political stability can be explained by the intelligence and resources possessed by political incumbents or by the apathy of the ruled masses.

The most obvious factor among the ruled that helps preserve political authority and diminishes mass-elite conflict is that most people are *politically apathetic*. In those countries in which voters have a choice of refraining from going to the polls, it is not at all unusual for one-third to one-half to remain at home. In the United States the percentage of those voting in recent presidential elections has varied from a low of fifty-one percent in 1948 to a high of sixty-four percent in 1968. In local elections voter turnouts are even lower. In Great Britain about seventy-five to eighty percent turn out for Parliamentary elections.

Such statistics indicate that substantial political apathy is characteristic of all political systems. Gabriel Almond and Sidney Verba surveyed citizen attitudes in five industrial democracies and found that a significant percentage of those interviewed pay no attention to political campaigns. The percentage paying no attention in each country varied from a low of twelve percent in the United States to a high of fifty-four percent in Italy. In addition, one-quarter of those interviewed in the United States reported that they never discuss politics with other people, compared with twenty-nine percent in Great Britain, thirty-nine percent in Germany, sixty-one percent in Mexico, and sixty-six percent in Italy.

Many people also reported feeling powerless to influence the political process. When asked if they thought they could influence the government to change a national law that they felt to be unjust, a substantial portion of those interviewed in all countries reported that they could not. The percentage varied from a high of seventy-two percent in Italy to a low of twenty-five percent in the United States. Even more significant, when citizens were asked *what they would do* to try and influence the national government, an average of nearly half of those interviewed said "nothing" or that they "didn't know," and only a minuscule percentage suggested some violent action as a means of protest.[10] Thus, a large portion of the citizenry in each country is not available for political mobilization and could hardly be expected to be supportive of political conflict.

The reasons that such large numbers fall into the ranks of the apathetic are not difficult to discern. Most people are too busy to take time to be informed about or actively to participate in politics and certainly are not likely to be mobilized by any political causes. They put in a long day at the factory or in the office and want to relax during leisure hours. They aren't about to ring doorbells for political candidates, to attend party caucuses, or engage in violent demonstrations. Most people are not potential revolutionaries; they simply want to be left alone.

These data reflect citizen beliefs and activities in five industrialized and democratic political systems. The level of political apathy is much higher in less industrial and less democratic countries. In traditional societies most people don't feel that they *should* actively participate in government or political affairs. People in the ruling class are considered to be superior, and questioning their authority is often proscribed by religious traditions. Although data are not available for less democratic countries, there are indications that high levels of political apathy and little sense of political efficacy exist there also. In the Soviet Union and other communist countries all those in good health *must* go to the polls on election day or face stiff fines, an indication that voter turnout might be embarrassingly low if citizens were permitted to remain home. Other studies, based largely on refugee interviews and personal experience, have indicated high levels of apathy and alienation in many countries that restrict political freedoms.[11]

The "costs" of active political participation also vary considerably among countries. In order to participate intelligently an individual must be educated and informed. Levels of education and availability of information vary among nations. Even a well-educated person in the Soviet Union, for example, does not normally have access to information needed to make informed political choices. A well-educated person in Great Britain, by contrast, has access to much information about political affairs at very low costs, that is, with little risk or effort.

There are other reasons that keep citizens from becoming "over-participatory" and attempting to topple ruling political elites. Robert Dahl has suggested three "criteria" for authority that help explain citizen support for privileged oligarchies in the absence of direct citizen participation in decision-making.[12] Perhaps the most important is the *criterion of competence*. Almost all people accept the competence of others to make decisions for them on some matters. If this weren't the case there would be no doctors, accountants, or pilots. For similar reasons people are willing to tolerate a small political oligarchy making decisions for the whole because, rightly or wrongly, ruling political elites are credited with more competence in political matters.

Dahl's second criterion for authority is that of *economy*. It is obviously impossible for every person in countries of substantial size to participate directly in central decision-making processes. While much has been made of the direct democracy of ancient Athens or of the New England town meeting, the number of eligible participants involved in these meetings was fairly small by contemporary standards. If all adults in the United States and Great Britain attempted to speak out and vote on all issues a cacophony of more than 100 million voices would result. Although futurists have suggested that computer terminals should some day be installed in homes for purposes of direct voting, the present system of delegating authority to the few to make decisions for the many is accepted by large majorities in almost all countries and is likely to persist for quite some time.

Efficiency and rationality are highly valued qualities in industrial societies and represent an important aspect of economy. Representation is efficient because small groups can effectively discuss, debate, and act quickly. Large groups are unwieldy, they procrastinate, and they frequently cannot take effective action even if consensus prevails. Rationality suggests respect for expertise and a division of labor in politics. Those most aware of and interested in certain problems may deal with them most effectively. Since most people neither have the time nor the desire to participate continuously in politics and since most people consider rationality, economy, and efficiency to be good things, political stability is preserved.

Dahl labels his third criterion for authority *personal choice*. Decisions made by ruling political elites do not correspond to the wishes of all of the people all of the time, but they do correspond to the choices of some of the people, usually the politically important people, on a fairly regular basis. Even in the most authoritarian political systems, ruling political elites do not recklessly disregard public opinion. In order to increase legitimacy, attempts are made by all political leaders *to appear* to be responding to citizen demands. Decisions made by ruling elites need not correspond to the personal choice of a majority, however, because not all citizens have equal political power and resources. It is the politically active and powerful who must be satisfied that decisions made correspond to *their* personal choice most of the time.

There is another important aspect of personal choice that explains persistence of regimes that sometimes make unpopular decisions. Even though present decisions that are made might not seem to be in an individual's interest, future decisions by future regimes might be. It is utilitarian to compromise and accept some decisions that may go against individual desires in the short run in the expectation that others will compromise when the situation is reversed. The alternative is frequent withdrawal from organized society and a return to a state of nature. Most people, particularly the politically influential, tolerate sometimes onerous decisions because they find anarchy and violence an unpleasant alternative, especially since their preferences prevail much of the time.

In summary, political stability can be maintained and mass-elite political conflict avoided because of several conditions that normally are found among those who are ruled. These include apathy, fed by lack of education and access to needed information, traditional beliefs that it is wrong for humble individuals to get involved in politics, and Dahl's criteria for delegating authority to smaller groups of ruling political elites: competence, economy, and personal choice.

Managing Political Conflict—The Rulers

In all organizations compliance is the essential element in relationships between those who have power and those over whom they exercise it.[13] In political systems, as in other organizational structures, maintaining continuing citizen obedience is essential to organization cohesion. No organization can reach its goals if members are pulling in different directions and habitually ignoring decisions made by the controlling oligarchy. An assembly line in a factory cannot function smoothly if workers do not follow instructions. Likewise, a political system cannot long survive as a cohesive and viable unit unless the majority of people are willing to continue to accept decisions reached by ruling political elites and obey prescribed laws.

Just as there are conditions among the ruled that help preserve stability, managerial actions of ruling political elites can either ensure continued citizen compliance and their own tenure in office or lead to their undoing. There are various aspects of ruling political elite power that can be combined in different strategies for managing potential conflict. When power is intelligently used, most people respond by obeying laws, and serious conflicts rarely develop. When the use of power is less than astute, social cohesion can wear thin and the legitimacy and authority of ruling elites is called into question.

One of the "rules" of politics that holds across time and cultures is that ruling political elites strive to remain in power once they obtain office. Whether elected, appointed, or self-appointed, ruling political elites rarely retire voluntarily. In authoritarian regimes aging dictators frequently use their political power to prevent "young turks" from replacing them. Thus, Mao Tse-tung in China, Joseph Stalin in the Soviet Union, Wladyslaw Gomulka in Poland, and Francisco Franco in Spain are all names that come to mind when thinking of leaders who have clung to or still cling to power well beyond normal retirement age. In the Soviet Union Stalin clung tenaciously to power for a quarter of a century before his death in 1953. Harold Lasswell attributes this phenomenon to a psychopathology that drives men to seek power and to attempt to maintain it once they get it.[14] Other reasons that ruling elites cling to power include vanity, ideology, habit, and undoubtedly a good measure of misguided altruism. Whatever the psychological mechanisms involved, once individuals become part of a ruling political elite they strive to maintain and use their power for as long as possible.

Democracies usually have a set of rules designed to deal with this problem, but they don't always work. Periodic elections, for example, are a vehicle for the peaceful replacement of aging political elites. In the United States, representatives serve terms of only two years and senators serve terms of six years. But desire to remain in power combined with great advantages accruing to incumbents has led to a situation in which many congressmen have served more than twenty-five consecutive years. Presidents have also been hesitant to leave office after only one four-year term. Franklin Roosevelt was serving his fourth term at the time of his death, Eisenhower served two terms, an unsuccessful war drove Lyndon Johnson from office after only five years and Richard Nixon was forced from office much against his will during his second term.

Ruling political elites in all political systems thus attempt to stem social and political conflict in order to enhance their chances of remaining in office. They use a variety of methods to exact citizen compliance. Sociologist Amitai Etzioni has outlined a "power-compliance" typology that is useful in understanding the various aspects of power that ruling political elites use. He labels these sets of strategies as *coercion, remuneration,* and *authority*.[15]

Coercion rests upon a monopoly of physical force that normally is in the hands of ruling political elites. Coercion is "the application, or threat of application, of physical sanctions. . . ."[16] The use of this aspect of power in gaining compliance is evidenced by torture, imprisonment, starvation, or even deaths of those who do not obey. Coercion is obviously not a preferred method of obtaining citizen compliance because, while it may win over the bodies of those to whom it is applied, it is counterproductive in winning over people's minds. Coercion is an expensive way of preserving law and order, both economically and in terms of citizen support. It costs money to maintain battle-ready troops, corrective facilities, and large police forces. It also chips away at regime legitimacy because the use of force is rarely considered by citizens to be morally good.

Remuneration means "control over material resources and rewards through allocations of salaries and wages, commissions and contributions, 'fringe benefits,' services and commodities . . ."—in other words, allocation of scarce positions and resources.[17] Political conflict can be reduced, social stability maintained, and compliance gained through intelligent distribution of social power, privilege, and prestige. Well-fed and socially satisfied people rarely engage in violence or revolution. Ability to use remunerative power is closely linked to economic performance; the more resources and positions that there are to allocate, the more effective remuneration can be as a managerial strategy. Remunerative power, therefore, is not reliable as it is dependent upon economic conditions that are sometimes beyond the control of political leaders. Depressions, resource shortages, inflation, and other forms of economic misery can severely limit remunerative power and, indirectly, political stability.

Authority, or normative power, rests on the "allocation and manipulation of symbolic rewards and deprivations. . . ."[18] It is the most desired aspect of power to exercise as it is relatively inexpensive and is very effective in eliciting citizen cooperation. Authority is an "internalized moral commitment to conform" and is quite different from obedience based on fear of sanctions.[19] Normative power can be exercised through manipulation of symbols and is enhanced by appeals to commonly held values. The use of this aspect of power is manifest in appeals to act in the name of "God, mother, or country."

Recourse to these different strategies for maintaining social and political stability leads to different political costs and creates different citizen orientations toward political authority. When individuals are coerced, obedience arises from fear of bodily harm and citizens become "alienated" from those doing the coercing. Thus, frequent use of troops to put down strikes may successfully disrupt such protests in the short run, but such methods of conflict management create resentment and a desire for revenge. The sight of flying police batons used against demonstrators undoubtedly radicalized more Americans during the late 1960s than did any of the anti-war literature of the period.

Remuneration leads to calculative citizen involvement as many see it to be in their self-interest to comply with laws. While not every person is an "economic man," making a daily calculation of gains and losses from supporting any particular political regime, economic progress is a cement that holds industrial societies together over the long-run. Abundance and progress lead to political stability and diminution of conflict because it is difficult for rebels to recruit people who have full stomachs. But this type of citizen involvement is less than ideal because it depends heavily upon continued betterment of economic conditions and increases in standards of living. That economic matters can often be beyond the control of ruling political elites was clearly demonstrated by the Arab embargo on oil shipments to many industrialized countries in 1973–74. The embargo and subsequent price increases triggered economic recessions, inflation, and serious political and social conflict in many countries. Similar economic conditions in Germany, resulting from the Great Depression, helped subvert established authorities and led to establishment of the Nazi Party as a potent political force. In the 1960s economic stagnation in Eastern Europe led to the ouster of Communist Party leaders Wladyslaw Gomulka in Poland and Antonin Novotny in Czechoslovakia. They were replaced by leaders promising various types of economic reform leading to greater abundance.

Use of normative power, or authority, represents an ideal managerial strategy when it can be successfully employed. People in all nations that endure for any length of time are held together by moral bonds that are rooted in sentiments, belief systems, and common wisdoms. Ruling political elites are supported by people who are convinced that existing laws are morally right. These people are committed to existing political regimes that they believe to be guardians of accepted moral values. Normative power is exercised through persuasion, and political conflict is managed by appealing to commonly held moral values.

In the complex real world different people obey laws and comply with orders of ruling political elites for different reasons and the combinations don't always fit neatly into Etzioni's abstract categories. Most people in the United States, for example, fill out fairly accurate income tax forms because they fear possible imprisonment (coercion) if they don't. But some also take economic penalties and fines for nonpayment into account (remuneration). There is a small and diminishing number of people who faithfully pay taxes because they believe it immoral or sinful to do otherwise (authority). Many obey speed laws because they fear arrest and detention. But some obey these laws because they wish to avoid paying fines or even because they calculate that it is in everyone's interest to drive at a safe speed. Some people also believe that to exceed speed limits is morally wrong. Reasons for compliance with laws also depend upon the particular issue involved. Most people refrain from murder because they believe it to be morally wrong, but they refrain from running stop signs because they are afraid of getting caught.

Ruling political elites are well aware of interpersonal differences in compliance behavior and the differential impact of various compliance-inducing techniques and they take these differences into account when making public policy. In some cases, traffic laws for example, decision-makers realize that only token compliance can be expected. Traffic fines have only a slight deterrent effect on most economic classes. Politicians also know that heavy fines or jail sentences for traffic violations are not likely to be tolerated by the public. Thus, modest noncompliance is often tolerated and government budgets frequently depend upon income from fines. Tacit approval of noncompliance and enforcement double standards are an important component of conflict management programs.

CREATING CITIZEN COMMITMENT

All ruling political elites have some capacity to use force to manage conflict. Otherwise they could not long remain in office. Substantial remunerative power is less frequently available, particularly in less economically developed countries. Normative power, based upon legitimacy, authority, and moral commitment to common goals, is the most desired type of power, and ruling elites continually attempt to buttress their authority and increase their ability to persuade. But since moral commitment to a political system or regime is built up only as a result of a history of positive experiences between rulers and ruled, political regimes in many countries face an uphill battle to establish authority.

In traditional societies authority has been closely tied to religious beliefs and defying rulers has been tantamount to defying God or gods. In medieval Europe, for example, the authority of the king was often buttressed with sermons of approval from bishops and cardinals. In many industrial countries, however, religion-anchored moral commitment is now on the wane and new types of political strategies are essential to the maintenance of citizen commitment.

Contemporary ruling political elites prefer to manage conflict through the use of moral suasion alone, but this is only possible when authority is unquestioned. Using persuasion is like spending money. As long as elites are perceived to be legitimate by those over whom they rule their persuasive "currency" is likely to be accepted. When there is little social, economic, or political cleavage very little currency need be expended. When the goals of ruling elites aren't congruent with those of the masses, however, or when various types of conflict threaten to divide society, currency must be continually expended to maintain stability. Karl Deutsch has equated the role of force in political crises to the role of gold in economic crises. "Physical force with its instrumentalities—men with tanks and guns—is a damage control mechanism of society. It can function as such a mechanism in situations where compliance with legal or political commands has broken down. . . ." "The tanks that [former French president] de Gaulle ordered into the streets of Paris on a critical day in early 1962 were thus analogous to the gold trucks conspicuously arriving at a bank threatened by panic among its depositors."[20] When authority begins to diminish regimes often attempt to inflate the value of their persuasive currency through information distortion and various types of propaganda. But information distortion cannot persist for long periods of time as officially painted views of the world are soon seen to be at variance from what people perceive to be taking place in the "real" world.

Such persuasive currency must be expended when political leaders attempt to reshape a nation's political culture, the set of political beliefs, expressive symbols, and values defining the situation within which politics takes place.[21] It is often necessary to reshape political cultures in economically developing countries where the goals and values of modernizing politicians and those of the traditional masses are sometimes incompatible. In such situations there are two different strategies by which goals and values may be made to seem more congruent and serious conflict thus avoided. The first is to invest heavily in *managing the flow of sociopolitical information* so that it appears that ruling political elites share the goals and values of the masses. The second strategy is to *modify individual belief systems* so that the goals and values of the masses actually do, over time, come to resemble those of the ruling elites.

Managing social information can involve directly censoring news, planting false statements in the mass media, faking results of public opinion polls, or a variety of other schemes. Information management is more easily accomplished in those countries in which the mass media are not highly developed. A small number of mass communication sources can be more easily controlled than can a more complex communications system. Furthermore, in less industrialized countries a significant proportion of the people does not have access to radio and television and is largely illiterate. Therefore, under these circumstances ruling political elites need worry about media manipulation for only a relatively small group of politically significant people.[22]

Industrialization and the associated development of "technetronic" societies, those in which beliefs are shaped by the impact of mass communications and electronics, give political regimes much greater potential for using electronic media and newspapers for image manipulation and creation of artificial bodies of social and political facts.[23] However, more literate and educated people are also more sophisticated in interpreting social, economic, and political facts outside the realm of immediate experience. There are many competing sources of information in technetronic societies, and it is therefore more difficult to maintain "closed" information systems. Thus, if ruling elites wish to manage effectively the flow of information in a highly industrialized society, a major investment of resources is required.

In authoritarian societies, such as Nazi Germany, entire ministries of communications and propaganda are or have often been devoted to the creation and dissemination of images corresponding to the wishes of politicians. The aim in Nazi Germany was to reduce internal conflict by directing aggression outward at enemies, real or fictitious.[24] During the communist revolutions in Eastern Europe following World War II, control of the ministries of interior and communications were the primary goals of revolutionaries. The former were the key to preserving stability through use of coercive power while the latter were critical to the exercise of persuasive power through image manipulation.

Although information management is not usually thought of as part of democratic politics, there is always tension between the open communication ideals of democracy and the realities of politics. Ruling political elites in democracies are no different from those in other political systems in their desire to manipulate the mass media into painting flattering pictures of them or their policies. These tendencies are normally restricted by democratic rules which forbid media censorship, as freedom of information is one of the cornerstones of democracy.

In democracies, however, politicians do their best to manage the media unobtrusively. The best recent example of tension between a free mass media and political desires to control information was the Nixon-Agnew assault on "media bias" in the United States in the late 1960s. The public, even though its trust in the media was somewhat shaken by the campaign, retained much more faith in the objectivity of the media than in the charges of politicians.

The second aspect of persuasion in maintaining authority is direct modification of citizen values, goals, and beliefs. Political socialization, the processes of internalizing a political culture, can be extremely important in creating a sense of community and in eliminating potential social and political conflict. Changing these basic values, beliefs, and expectations as they relate to politics is a very difficult task. Even in technetronic societies, basic political values and beliefs seem to change only slowly over several generations. The ideological content of most political party platforms in industrial democracies, for example, was basically established in the 1930s and hasn't changed much since then. Neither has the base of support for these parties.[25] When major efforts to modify belief structures are made by political leaders they are usually directed toward the formative years of younger generations.

Sociopolitical values are learned through interactions with primary and secondary agents of socialization. Primary agents include the family, the childhood peer group, or certain religious organizations. Secondary agents of socialization are much more numerous and include political parties, labor unions, social clubs, etc. The main difference between primary and secondary agents of socialization is that involvement with the former is total and emotional whereas involvement with the latter is partial and utilitarian. For example, people internalize the norms and values of primary groups (agents) for *moral* reasons that have roots in individuals' needs to be accepted by groups. Individuals internalize *some* of the norms of secondary groups only because they *calculate* it to be in their own interest to do so. Quite naturally, primary groups are much more effective agents of socialization than are secondary groups.[26]

Political socialization in primary groups is more covert than overt. Parents, for example, generally do not pass on political attitudes to their children by means of nightly patriotism lessons at the dining room table. Rather, children pick up cues from parents and peer groups and internalize the attitudes and emulate the behavior of others. Attitude formation related to politics thus takes place informally in primary groups.

Secondary agents of socialization are more numerous, but their impact on political attitude formation is not as great. Since these relationships are of an instrumental nature (labor unions basically interested in wages, political parties in electing candidates, social clubs in preserving the neighborhood), they are not particularly important in influencing values and attitudes outside of the narrow sphere with which they are concerned. Personal involvement with secondary groups is limited in duration, utilitarian in purpose, and less important to an individual than are primary relationships. Therefore, political socialization within secondary groups must be conscious and overt since members are not likely to be influenced in other ways by groups to which there is little commitment.

Intervention in socialization processes poses a great many difficulties as well as opportunities for political incumbents. The most effective agents of socialization, those with which an individual has affective, primary-type involvements, are the most difficult for political regimes to influence and manipulate. Although there were scattered reports of children turning against parents during the heights of mobilization campaigns in the Soviet Union and Communist China, the family is normally a very cohesive unit and is not easily disrupted by political forces. Development of peer group norms and values is very difficult for ruling political elites to control. Penetration and control of secondary relationships is much more easily accomplished, but, because of their instrumental nature, such penetration and control can be so ineffective in changing values as to make the effort hardly worthwhile.[27]

Thus, whether an attempt is made to change citizen attitudes, values, and beliefs to diminish elite-mass conflict or various forms of existing socioeconomic conflict, elite intervention in political socialization is a dubious proposition. Normally, ruling political elites in democracies fairly accurately reflect the values and aspirations of those who elect them. But on certain critical issues political leaders must assert their leadership. Racial prejudice is an obvious example. Such attempts may very well be futile since all the "sanitized" and "approved" schoolbooks in the world may not overcome prejudices learned in the home or within the peer group. At best, authority can be enhanced through regime efforts to control political socialization only by means of sustained efforts across many generations. Basic attitudes, values, and beliefs cannot be altered in periods of weeks, months, or even years.

Industrialization, Stability, Democracy

Industrialization and related economic development has a great impact on the nature of compliance relationships. Economic development represents one of those favorable experiences that enhances regime authority and legitimacy. Development also creates new positions and resources that can be allocated by ruling political elites and thus creates an opportunity to augment remunerative power and calculative citizen involvement. As societies become more economically developed coercion normally plays a much smaller role as a managerial tool.

Industrialization and economic development are accompanied by changes in political relationships that are referred to as political development. But there is no scholarly agreement on what constitutes political development. The simplest, and perhaps most ethnocentric, attempt to define political development equates it with the democratic institutions and political participation that have developed in the United States and Great Britain.[28] Others have been more concerned with national integration, political participation, and increasing institutional rationalization.[29] Perhaps the most useful approach to political development defines it as a relationship, balancing the types of challenges to authority posed by industrialization against the increased power of ruling political elites to deal with these challenges.[30] All of these definitions of political development generally include some form of established authority, democratic participation, and political stability as criteria for denoting politically developed nations. Given the great interest in cross-national studies of political development and violence as well as in various strategies of political conflict management, a considerable body of literature now exists relating changing socioeconomic conditions to aspects of political development.

Seymour Martin Lipset was one of the earliest scholars to examine empirically these relationships. Lipset implicitly accepted political stability and democracy as definitions of political development. He was interested in pinpointing the socioeconomic requisites for stability and democracy and he used a wealth of socioeconomic and political data on individual countries to make comparisons. Lipset arranged his socioeconomic data under four different headings: indicators of national wealth, industrialization, education, and urbanization. Because of great difficulties in collecting enough data to rank countries adequately according to levels of democracy or political stability, he again used only four categories of countries. He first separated European and English-speaking democracies. He then further divided them into those which he perceived to be stable democracies and those which he perceived to be unstable democracies or dictatorships. He also compared a group of Latin American countries and divided them into two similar groups: those that he perceived to be democracies and unstable dictatorships and those perceived to be stable dictatorships.

Although by contemporary standards Lipset's methods and measurements seem rough and crude, he first systematically illustrated that there are great social and economic differences among his categories of political systems. In stable Latin American dictatorships, for example, he found an average of ten telephones per one-thousand people, an average literacy rate of only forty-six percent, very low energy usage per capita, and very low levels of urbanization. In Latin American democracies and unstable dictatorships, representing what he considered to be more politically developed countries, he found an average of twenty-five telephones per one-thousand people, an average literacy rate of seventy-five percent, relatively high levels of per capita energy consumption, and relatively high levels of urbanization.

The contrast was even greater when these countries were compared with stable European democracies. Lipset found over two-hundred telephones per thousand people, an average literacy rate of ninety-six percent, and very high levels of energy consumption per capita and urbanization in European countries. By using these crude methods of comparison, Lipset inferred that industrialization, political stability, and democracy are related through a series of mediating variables that are part of a general developmental process. He considered some of these variables to be increasing levels of income, higher levels of security, and more public education. Wealthier persons, he reasoned, were more likely to be satisfied with living conditions and have more to lose in violent political struggles. Class conflict also is less important in industrial countries as apparent gaps between rich and poor seem to decrease. Greater wealth and income increase exposure to "cross pressures" (membership and stakes in many different organizations) and these reduce commitment to ideologies and make people less responsive to extremist movements.[31]

Sociologist Phillips Cutright built upon Lipset's work by constructing a detailed index of political development. According to Cutright, a politically developed nation has "more complex and specialized national political institutions."[32] Cutright found that political institutions are influenced by educational systems, economic development, communications systems, and urbanization. There was a very high correlation among these various indicators of socioeconomic development and his index of political development. Those countries with highly developed systems of mass communications, high levels of urbanization, and high levels of education, were usually those countries that were more politically developed according to Cutright's definitions.

Many others have further refined Lipset's work and probed relationships similar to those that he studied. In my own work, for example, a positive relationship was found among indicators of economic development, as measured by gross national product per capita, and "non-coercive compliance structures" and elite "responsiveness" to citizen demands in a sample of thirty-five countries.[33]

A question that arises from this line of study is whether highly industrial countries necessarily become *more* democratic and stable as they reach industrial maturity. In other words, is there a threshold beyond which industrial nations no longer become more democratic and politically stable? Dean Neubauer addressed himself to this question in a study of democratic performance in highly industrialized countries.[34] In order to test his hypotheses, Neubauer devised a much more complex index of democratic performance than did Cutright. According to this more sophisticated measure, the relationship between industrialization and many aspects of democracy is much weaker at advanced levels of industrial development. The United States, for example, ranked highest in level of industrialization, but only sixteenth on the scale of democratic performance. Furthermore, Neubauer found that there was little correlation between a nation's rank on his index and on Cutright's scale of political development.

Communist countries represent an anomaly for those engaged in this line of research dealing with economic development, democracy, and political stability. Many communist party states are industrially developed; most are politically stable, but they can hardly be classified as democracies. My own work applying Lipset-type hypotheses to communist countries revealed that there is no relationship between industrialization and democracy or liberalization in the Communist Bloc. Czechoslovakia and East Germany are by far the most industrially developed communist countries, but they rank seventh and eighth out of nine communist countries on a liberalization index. Yugoslavia (low levels of industrialization) and Poland (intermediate levels) rank first and second. These facts obviously call for additional interpretation if they are to fit into a more general theory relating economic development, democracy, and stability.

Industrialization leads to pressures for political participation. Regimes can respond to these pressures or use force in combination with some type of remuneration to maintain control in the absence of citizen commitment that would normally result from more democratic participation. In industrialized communist countries, when citizens and ruling political elites have not been engaged in mutually satisfactory participation relationships, economic development is adversely affected by citizen disenchantment and sporadic outbursts of political violence related to citizen dissatisfaction are likely. In brief, political leaders in those countries that don't "fit" the industrialization-stabilization-democracy model are forced to expend scarce political "currency" in coping with substantial pressure for greater political participation.

History has validated this line of thinking. Pressures for meaningful participation and a serious crisis in economic production in Czechoslovakia in the mid 1960s led to the replacement of the coercive regime of Antonin Novotny with a more responsive regime under Alexander Dubcek. But Soviet intervention soon resulted in another regime heavily dependent upon coercive force which was augmented by Soviet troops. Similarly, economic and political discontent in Poland in the late 1960s, based partially on lack of elite responsiveness to worker demands and in part on citizen dissatisfaction with economic conditions, led to the ouster of Wladyslaw Gomulka and his replacement by Edward Gierek. For reasons that could be related to a heritage of "Prussian" political culture, only East Germany remains an authoritarian industrialized communist party state that has not recently experienced significant economic difficulties or violence related to citizen discontent.

In summary, this line of empirical inquiry into relationships among industrialization, political stability, and democracy has yielded much valuable knowledge about mass-elite relationships and social and political conflict related to national socioeconomic development. There is a clear relationship among measures of industrial development, democracy, and political stability. The managerial strategies used by ruling political elites and their successes or failures in managing conflict and increasing authority at different levels of economic development and under different sociopolitical conditions are discussed in the following chapters.

REFERENCES

1. R. Michels, *Political Parties.* New York: Free Press, 1958, pp. 393–409.
2. See G. Almond and G. Powell, *Comparative Politics: A Developmental Approach.* Boston: Little, Brown, 1966, pp. 47–48.
3. R. Gregg and A. Banks, "Dimensions of Political Systems: Factor Analysis of a Cross-Polity Survey," *The American Political Science Review* (September 1965).
4. K. Prewitt and A. Stone, *The Ruling Elites: Elite Theory, Power*

and American Democracy. New York: Harper and Row, 1973, p. 137.
5. C. W. Mills, *The Power Elite.* New York: Oxford University Press, 1956; G. Domhoff, *Who Rules America?* Englewood Cliffs, N.J.: Prentice-Hall, 1967. See also G. Domhoff and H. Ballard, eds., *C. Wright Mills and the Power Elite.* Boston: Beacon Press, 1968.
6. See P. Bachrach, *The Theory of Democratic Elitism: A Critique.* Boston: Little, Brown, 1967, ch. 4.
7. G. Mosca, *The Ruling Class.* New York: McGraw-Hill, 1939; V. Pareto, *The Mind and Society.* New York: Dover, 1963; P. Bachrach, *The Theory of Democratic Elitism,* ch. 2. See also S. Keller, *Beyond the Ruling Class.* New York: Random House, 1963, chs. 1 and 2.
8. See M. Knight, *The German Executive, 1890–1933.* Stanford, Calif.: The Hoover Institution, 1952.
9. H. Eckstein, "On the Etiology of Internal Wars," in I. Feierabend, R. Feierabend, and T. Gurr, eds., *Anger, Violence, and Politics: Theories and Research.* Englewood Cliffs, N.J.: Prentice-Hall, 1972.
10. G. Almond and S. Verba, *The Civic Culture.* Boston: Little, Brown, 1965, ch. 6.
11. A. Inkeles and R. Bauer, *The Soviet Citizen.* New York: Atheneum, 1968, chs. 10 and 11.
12. R. Dahl, *After the Revolution?: Authority in a Good Society.* New Haven: Yale University Press, 1970, pp. 8–56.
13. See G. Simmel, "Superiority and Subordination as a Subject-Matter of Sociology," *American Journal of Sociology* 2 (1896).
14. H. Lasswell, *Psychopathology and Politics.* New York: Viking, 1960.
15. A. Etzioni, *A Comparative Analysis of Complex Organizations.* New York: Free Press, 1961, pp. 4–6.
16. Etzioni, *A Comparative Analysis of Complex Organizations,* p. 5.
17. Etzioni, *A Comparative Analysis of Complex Organizations,* p. 5.
18. Etzioni, *A Comparative Analysis of Complex Organizations,* p. 5.
19. J. Gilison, *British and Soviet Politics: Legitimacy and Convergence.* Baltimore: The Johns Hopkins University Press, 1972, p. 7.
20. K. Deutsch, *The Nerves of Government.* New York: Free Press, 1963, p. 122.
21. See S. Verba, "Comparative Political Culture," in L. Pye and S. Verba, eds., *Political Culture and Political Development.* Princeton: Princeton University Press, 1965.
22. The reverse, however, is also true. Without effective communication it is difficult for ruling political elites to penetrate and mobilize a society.
23. Z. Brzezinski, *Between Two Ages: America's Role in the Technetronic Era.* New York: Viking, 1970, p. 9.

24. D. Finlay, O. Holsti, and R. Fagen, *Enemies in Politics*. Chicago: Rand McNally, 1967, ch. 1.
25. S. M. Lipset and S. Rokkan, eds., *Party Systems and Voter Alignments*. New York: Free Press, 1967, Introduction.
26. See D. Jaros, *Socialization to Politics*. New York: Praeger, 1973, chs. 4–6.
27. See D. Pirages, *Modernization and Political-Tension Management: A Socialist Society in Perspective*. New York: Praeger, 1972, ch. 3.
28. R. Packenham, "Approaches to the Study of Political Development," *World Politics* (October 1964): 108–10.
29. G. Almond and J. Coleman, eds., *The Politics of Developing Areas*. Princeton: Princeton University Press, 1960, pp. 532–33.
30. S. Huntington, "Political Development and Political Decay," *World Politics* (April 1965); S. Huntington, *Political Order in Changing Societies*. New Haven: Yale University Press, 1968.
31. S. M. Lipset, *Political Man: The Social Bases of Politics*. New York: Doubleday, 1960, ch. 2.
32. P. Cutright, "National Political Development: Measurement and Analysis," in C. Cnudde and D. Neubauer, eds., *Empirical Democratic Theory*. Chicago: Markham, 1969, p. 195.
33. D. Pirages, "Socioeconomic Development and Political Access in the Communist Party States," in J. Triska, ed., *Communist Party States: Comparative and International Studies*. Indianapolis: Bobbs-Merrill, 1969.
34. D. Neubauer, "Some Correlates of Democracy," *American Political Science Review* (December 1967).

3

POLITICAL CONFLICT IN DEVELOPING COUNTRIES

Modernization is a term that describes a great number of changes in social organization resulting from the increasing task specialization and structural differentiation that accompanies industrialization. It refers to the cluster of economic, social, psychological, and political phenomena that are linked to an increasingly complex organization of industrial production. Economically, modernization means application of new technologies to productive processes in order to bring about great increases in human productivity. Sociologically, modernization denotes increased differentiation of social structures and the formation of new social institutions. Politically, modernization leads to the evolution of highly differentiated and specialized political institutions, an increased role for bureaucracy, and greater demands for political participation.[1]

Industrialization is the essential component of modernization and provides an impetus for the transformation of agricultural societies. Industrialization is based upon *substitution of inanimate forms of energy*—wind, water, coal, petroleum, natural gas, etc.—for energy formerly supplied by man and beast. Industrialization is also based on *economies of scale* in production and distribution. In preindustrial economies, production of goods is in the hands of individual skilled craftsmen and artisans, each one of whom is responsible for shaping a complete product. Economies of scale mean centralization of production activities in urban areas and the integration of peripheral regions into larger systems of distribution. In industrial societies the artisan gives way to the factory and the assembly line. Industrialization and the associated division of labor, job specialization, transition from small units of production and distribution to mass production, large-scale marketing, and mass consumption lead to increasing levels of economic affluence.

Karl Deutsch has coined the term *social mobilization* to describe what takes place when modernization is compressed into a relatively short period of time. According to Deutsch mobilization is "the process in which major clusters of old social, economic, and psychological commitments are eroded and broken and people become available for new patterns of socialization and behavior."[2] In rapidly modernizing societies a substantial portion of the population is in transition both psychologically and geographically as allegiances shift from smaller groups of a "primordial" nature, such as family, clan, village, caste, or tribe, to larger, more centralized national organizations representing modern and secular perspectives.[3] Social mobilization means exposure of many persons to an industrial way of life as they move from country to city and assume new economic roles in an industrializing economy.

Modernization has important psychological components that parallel geographic, economic, social, and political changes. Exposure to books, newspapers, electronic media, urban culture, movies, etc. increases individual "psychic mobility" and raises socioeconomic and political expectations. The peasant in traditional societies lives in an unchanging village environment. Modernization systematically destroys this traditional way of life. Modern individuals are ready for new experiences and are much more open to innovation and change than are their traditional counterparts. They are not afraid of experimentation and are more willing to try new technologies, such as birth control devices, antibiotics, or methods of farming. Modern people also develop an ability to form opinions on issues transcending the village environment. Daniel Lerner has used the term "empathy" to describe this ability of individuals to imagine themselves in the places of distant others and to take positions on issues that do not necessarily have an immediate impact on village life.[4]

Many social scientists have attempted to define more clearly this psychological cluster of changes that accompanies industrial development and social modernization. Among these are Alex Inkeles,[5] Joseph Kahl,[6] Leonard Doob,[7] and Robert Clark.[8] The most significant agreement found among these researchers is on the proposition that a modern individual feels that *human beings can triumph over nature* whereas a traditional person feels constrained by forces beyond his or her control. Psychologically modern individuals think that nature can be controlled; that it is wise to build sewage systems, flood control dams, water purification plants, to use fertilizers, and to engage in family planning. This is closely related to feelings of "political efficacy," beliefs that through politics collective welfare can be influenced by human efforts.

Respect for the opinions of others is also an important part of modernization. The modern individual is willing to listen to others and to entertain new ideas. The traditional individual, by contrast, is more likely to "know" the truth and maintain a closed mind toward new ideas. This is closely linked to another proposition on which there is general agreement. Modern individuals have a *need to associate with others*. They join groups and interact in group settings much more frequently than do traditionals. They also have a *greater level of trust* in other people.

There is less, but still significant agreement on five other psychological aspects of modernization. These include *faith in science and technology* and a belief that the world is rational and can be controlled by human beings. This is accompanied by a *future orientation toward life* which is related to the ability to defer immediate gratification for long-term gains. This attribute, of course, is central to industrialization since investment capital for future development can be obtained only by foregoing consumption in the present. In addition, modern individuals *feel traditional institutional pressures less frequently, have stronger egos* than do traditionals, and *are basically optimistic* about life and the future.[9]

Modern individuals contrast strongly with traditionals on all of these psychological dimensions of modernization. Politically this can lead to very different perceptions of national needs and policy demands from different segments of a population depending upon their ages and geographic location. Those who stay behind in villages and those who mentally or geographically migrate to an industrial way of life have basically different views of the world. Modernization creates psychological stress and social conflict that spills over into politics because fundamental value questions must be resolved. Traditional leaders, for example, may oppose a modern school system on the grounds that it could erode religious customs and encourage women to step out of line. Traditionals might also oppose democratic elections on the grounds that such political activities are not in keeping with the will of "the gods" who, of course, have specified that traditional authorities should be the repositories of political wisdom! These psychological dramas accompanying industrialization have been played out over many generations in today's industrial countries, and these slower transitions to modernity can profitably be studied to gain a better understanding of the types of conflicts involved. Many contemporary modernizing nations are now confronting many of these problems simultaneously, and studying the resulting conflicts increases our understanding of problems of conflict management.

Historical Patterns of Industrialization and Conflict

Since its hesitant beginnings in fifteenth- and sixteenth-century England, industrialization and the associated economic development and social modernization has greatly influenced the structure of societies and the nature of political systems everywhere. However, of the more than 150 national units that now exist, only about twenty qualify as being highly industrialized. The vast majority are countries in transition, moving from agricultural to more industrial ways of life. In most of these countries legitimacy, authority, democracy, and political stability exist only as goals for the distant future.

The dynamics of industrialization spread outward from England to the rest of the world, courtesy of merchants, missionaries, and the military. Industrialization has reshaped the nature of economic, social, and political life in the countries affected. The political stability and mass democracy that are characteristic of some contemporary industrialized societies are the products of a series of unique modernization-related historical sequences that followed industrialization. Contemporary dictatorships and political instability in other countries can be explained by different responses to industrialization and less successful historical interactions between ruling political elites and the politically active segments of society.

Almost all contemporary industrial countries have checkered histories filled with periods of violence, political instability, and authoritarian rule accompanying the transformation of agricultural societies into industrial ones. Analyzing the spread or *diffusion* of industrialization and related political ideas can broaden perspective on industrialization, conflict, and conflict management in contemporary developing nations.

The impact of industrialization on national political units has been analytically divided into four aspects: state-building, nation-building, demands for political participation, and demands for redistribution of economic resources.[10] These tasks and challenges have been faced in those countries that industrialized very early and they are presently being faced by political leaders in those countries that are still modernizing.

State-Building. Preindustrial political units are usually very small, widely dispersed, and semiautonomous. Largely because of primitive methods of transportation and communication, it is difficult for centralizing political leadership to maintain a high degree of political control over smaller, peripheral units. Thus, primitive kingdoms or empires have usually consisted of coalitions of smaller political systems only loosely knit together into a larger whole. Relations between centralizing leadership and traditional leaders on the periphery have fluctuated over time and have been closely related to the aggressiveness, skill, coercive power, and the territorial designs of central authorities.[11] In medieval England, for example, centralizing leadership was represented by the king, and his vassals represented the periphery. The vassals were often given (or took) great liberties in controlling their allotted territory. Stability under the feudal system was achieved through a system of reciprocal ties. A vassal swore fealty to a ruler and in return the ruler granted a fief. These grants usually included vassal immunity for his acts within the political unit that was held in fief. This arrangement represented a method of delegating authority and tacit recognition of the dispersal of political power and the inability of the king to rule vast territories effectively.[12]

State-building involves the process of penetrating these peripheral political systems and integrating them into a larger and more centralized state. It means destroying the politics of localism and making citizens subject to central authority, a process that is often filled with conflict. State-building "occurs when the [ruling] political elite creates new structures and organizations designed to 'penetrate' the society in order to regulate behavior in it and draw a larger volume of resources from it."[13] These new structures include development of a centralized and effective bureaucracy capable of maintaining order.

State-building can only take place when centralizing political leaders have the wherewithal to maintain order in areas they have penetrated. This has been true in the historical development of England, France, and Germany, just as it is true in China, India, or Nigeria today. The industrial revolution has provided an important impetus for state-building because it has created the communication, transportation, and military infrastructures required to maintain order over large stretches of territory. But threats from other countries, internal military conflict, the ambitions of political authorities, or even "manifest destiny" have also acted and can now act as catalysts in state-building.

Nation-Building. Nation-building frequently accompanies state-building but should be viewed as a separate process. Nation-building "refers to the process whereby people transfer their commitment and loyalty from smaller tribes, villages, or petty principalities to the larger central political system."[14] Even though national boundaries may be established and the power of centralizing political elites may be unquestioned, there is no guarantee that national unity follows. In fact, there are many cases, including the Austro-Hungarian Empire, Yugoslavia, Ireland, Cyprus, Nigeria, etc., where boundaries of recognized states have not or do not correspond to the boundaries of citizen loyalties or commitment. A nation can only be built when a feeling of covariance exists as a result of well-developed social communication. If there is no "in-group" identification or "we" feeling a state may very well exist but a nation is yet to be built.

One of the best ways to test whether a nation has been built is to ask of the inhabitants of a country "what are you?" In the United States there is little doubt that most people would answer "I am an American." Similarly, in Great Britain most people would answer "I am British." But in Nigeria a large part of the population would undoubtedly answer "I am Ibo" rather than "I am Nigerian." In Nigeria and many other less industrial countries, national borders have been determined by external forces and encompass many nationalities and groupings that do not work well together and have not yet been effectively integrated into national political life. In some cases geographical boundaries of a state encompass so many different ethnic groups or tribes that building an integrated nation might be impossible.

Citizen Demands. Historically, questions of political participation and distribution of welfare became serious issues only after state-building and nation-building had been successfully carried out. This is particularly true in those countries that eventually developed democracy and stable authority relationships and where integration of peripheral areas into the political mainstream and a well-developed sense of national unity existed long before demands for political participation or redistribution became overwhelming. Thus, the challenges to ruling political elites resulting from modernization were not cumulative, and substantial periods of time were available to resolve each set of problems sequentially.

T. H. Marshall has analyzed the way in which demands for citizenship, political participation, and social welfare developed in Great Britain only after the strife that accompanied state- and nation-building had been resolved.[15] According to Marshall there is a basic conflict between social class and citizenship rights. Social class represents an organized system of inequality whereas citizenship bestows a variety of equal rights and privileges on those who qualify. Therefore, it is only natural that privileged classes have historically resisted the extension of citizenship, the vote, and basic social rights to those of lesser status. Marshall has pointed out that the class battle over civil, political, and then social rights in England took place over a long time and in sequence, and that this permitted peaceful compromise of potentially dangerous disputes and the emergence of democracy.

New civil rights were first added to those few individual rights that survived after the breakdown of the feudal system. The most important aspect of the extension of these citizenship rights was that for the first time all men were to be guaranteed equal rights under the law, something that the privileged classes found difficult to accept. Later these civil rights would apply to women as well.

The struggle over the spread of political rights did not begin in England until most civil rights controversies had been resolved. In the case of the right to vote no novel privileges were created. Existing rights for the wealthy were simply extended to others increasingly distant from centers of power. This occurred during the latter part of the nineteenth century, as the right to vote was extended to those of lesser and lesser economic substance. The impetus for such action was a combination of pressures from those demanding the right to vote and from politicians expecting to profit from the granting of such rights to new constituencies.

The lessons learned from the British experience, and to a lesser extent experiences of other European industrial democracies, are that political stability can be maintained, social violence minimized, and democratic political systems established in situations in which crises of state- and nation-building, participation, and welfare do not become cumulative and where there is plenty of time available.

There are many other factors that have been identified through historical analysis as being important in determining patterns of contemporary political stability, violence, and types of authority relationships in industrial societies. Barrington Moore, Jr., for example, has found that the economic position of the peasantry, the development of entrepreneurial attitudes among a landed upper class, the nature of relationships between a developing urban bourgeoisie and a landed upper class and the various combinations of economic interests holding political power have been important in determining the political paths followed as nations industrialized. He has outlined three different routes from the preindustrial to the modern world: one leading to bourgeois revolution and democracy, one to control from above and fascism, and one to peasant revolution leading to communism.[16]

The first route, leading to stability and democracy, is characterized by a combination of rural capitalism, a strong urban industrial class, and a parliamentary democracy controlled by coalitions of landowners and urban commercial interests. In the sixteenth and seventeenth centuries royal absolutism and agrarian bureaucracies were found in almost all Western European countries, Russia, China, Japan, and India. In those countries in which a revolutionary struggle to check arbitrary rulers took place early, the outcome was generally favorable to contemporary stability and democracy. In England it was the Puritan Revolution and in France it was the French Revolution that destroyed royal absolutism and paved the way for the growth of bourgeois democracy. Where various forms of absolutism and agrarian bureaucracy persisted into the twentieth century (China, Russia), the outcomes were less favorable to democracy.[17]

According to Moore, the development of fascism and communism has sprung from similar sets of historical circumstances. A landed upper class has often kept peasants tied to the land under "labor repressive" conditions with the help of authoritarian rulers. A landed aristocracy, buttressed by authoritarian rulers, may combine forces with a commercial and industrial class that is too weak to seize power in its own right. This combination of royal bureaucracy, powerful landed aristocracy, and a weak commercial class aligned against an oppressed peasantry has resulted in various forms of fascism and authoritarian forms of government associated with violence and repression. If an agrarian aristocracy aligns itself with absolutist power and manages to thwart industrialization, leaving the peasants on the land under impoverished conditions, the eventual result is likely to be political violence resulting in some type of communist revolution.[18]

Historical sequences of development, old social cleavages, religious problems, regional antagonisms, patterns of industrialization, and historical compromises have all played an important role in shaping contemporary politics and serve as partial explanations for existing conflict and authority problems in all contemporary political systems. Recurring political instability in France, for example, can be partially attributed to incomplete industrialization and a failure to urbanize and develop commercial agriculture. A pattern of arbitrary politics in the Soviet Union was set long ago under the Czars because no industrializing bourgeois arose to challenge their power.

This perspective can also contribute to analysis of prospects for democracy and political stability in today's developing countries. In general, the odds are not good. De Schweinitz has concluded an historical analysis of relationships between industrialization and political development with an observation that in those countries where the industrial revolution had a profound effect (Great Britain, the United States) stable democracies developed. European countries least affected by the industrial revolution (Spain, Portugal, the USSR) retained authoritarian and unstable governments.[19] De Schweinitz argues that industrialization resulting in transitions to pluralist democracies historically took place at the initiative of individuals and groups that were able to develop entrepreneurial activity separate from the state. Democracy has been "historically stimulated by the independent growth of the entrepreneurial and laboring classes which placed persistent and ineluctable demands on non-democratic political leaders for the extension of political rights."[20] De Schweinitz concludes by arguing that in contemporary developing countries the impetus for economic growth frequently comes from an authoritarian government, and the growth of any autonomous centers of economic power is thwarted. A unique configuration of conditions including availability of natural resources, mobility of populations, democratic ideologies, and unique loci and sequences of political development accounts for the emergence of democracy in the nineteenth century. Similar conditions do not exist in the twentieth century and it is unlikely that they will develop in the future.[21]

Authority and Conflict in Developing Countries

Industrial culture with its associated social and political changes spread outward from England slowly, and most contemporary industrial democracies had long periods of time in which to work out the problems of authority and instability that result from the industrialization process. In England the transformation of a largely agrarian society into one dominated by factory smokestakes took centuries. Industrialization in the United States was accomplished over an extended period in the nineteenth and twentieth centuries when there were few other industrial democracies to serve as examples and when the rate at which new ideas were diffused from one society to another was very low.

Contemporary leaders in the world's less-industrialized countries, however, are faced with a situation in which intense economic growth and accompanying social mobilization are telescoped into only one or two generations. An exponential growth in the rate of social change has resulted from a revolution in global communication and a more rapid dissemination of new ideas. Emergence of this "global village" means much more exposure of people in less-developed countries to the economic and political luxuries that have resulted from generations of slow evolution in presently industrialized countries.

Industrialization and modernization have become priority goals in almost all of the world's less-developed countries. Modernization is triggered by desires for economic progress which have been introduced by contact with economically more advanced cultures. Ruling political elites press for economic progress because, in Mack and Snyder's terminology, industrialization creates new resources and positions that can be used in managing conflict and in stemming a revolution of rising expectations thereby increasing political stability.

From a conflict management perspective the economic benefits of modernization cannot be easily severed from other aspects that are less desired. Industrialization is tied to *structural differentiation* and *task specialization*. Modernization transforms homogeneous peasant societies into complex societies characterized by division of labor, development of occupational groups and classes, large-scale social and political organization, political parties, interest groups, etc. This transformation is accompanied by shifts in expectations and values as well as by changes in the nature of social and political institutions. All of these changes exact a tremendous human toll as people adjust to new values and practices. For this reason, ruling political elites often attempt to sever industrialization from its non-economic component. The number of successes, however, has been extremely limited.

Economic, social, and political changes generate psychological stress which results in social and political instability. The introduction of new concepts and institutions that have developed over long periods of time in other cultural settings can create *cognitive dissonance* within transitional populations. Cognitive dissonance occurs when there is incongruence between the internalized images of the socioeconomic world and the world that actually exists. Other types of stress are caused by feelings of *relative deprivation* (a term used to describe discrepancies between the perceived "ought" and the perceived "is" of collective value satisfaction) which is related to rising expectations that cannot be met within existing structures of opportunity. Stress leads to frustration and violence which is often manifest in political instability.[22] In Indonesia stress resulting from competing value systems led to the massacre in 1965 of hundreds of thousands of communists and their sympathizers at the hands of more traditional Hindus. In Chile, similar frustrations were vented against communists in a much more limited bloodbath after the fall of Salvadore Allende in 1973. In many such cases the dissonance introduced by rapid change in values becomes unendurable, and once the stretched social fabric snaps, those individuals who have experienced mental discomfort often wreak vengeance on those whom they consider to be responsible.

The wide variety of causes of conflict resulting from the stress of modernization cannot easily be divided into categories. Riggs has suggested that modernization itself can result either from *endogenous* (internal) or *exogenous* (external) stimuli.[23] In keeping with this type of dichotomy the causes of political conflict in developing areas can be divided into those that are endogenous and those that are exogenous. Examples of endogenous factors would be conflict resulting from tensions among tribes or castes, among religious groupings, or among those profiting from economic modernization and those profiting from traditional ways of doing things. An example of an exogenous factor would be conflict generated by the diffusion of participatory ideologies to those areas of the world that are not yet politically ready for such developments.

In keeping with Eckstein's suggestion that too much attention has been concentrated upon rebels and too little has been paid to those being rebelled against, endogenous causes of conflict may be further divided into *conflict generated by incumbents* and *conflict generated by insurgents*. Studies of modernization and political development are top heavy with references to stress undergone by the masses during modernization but few references are made to the ruling elite and the successes and failures of their conflict management tactics. Eckstein suggests that explanations for internal wars may well be found in elite characteristics alone. "A ruling elite may decay, may become torn by severe conflict, may be reluctant to use power, may come to lack vital political skills—and thus make it possible for a relatively weak, even disorganized, opposition of a sort that may exist in any political system to rise against it and destroy it."[24]

Exogenous Sources of Conflict. The process by which innovations and ideas spread to members of a social system is called "diffusion." Rogers and Shoemaker have divided diffusion of ideas into two categories: *homophily*, the transfer of ideas among individuals of similar backgrounds, and *heterophily*, the transfer of ideas among individuals with different backgrounds.[25] Heterophilous diffusion of innovations from industrial societies to developing areas is one of the most important *exogenous causes of political conflict*. Ideas can be very important in creating discontent and there are many vehicles by which they travel. Sometimes these diffused ideas fit easily into cultures into which they are introduced but many times they do not.

One vehicle by which political ideas have been transferred from industrial countries to developing areas has been through colonial power-colony relationships. In some countries the transfer of Western-style bureaucracy and democratic political processes has been relatively successful. In others it has been a failure. In Africa, for example, those countries formerly under British rule have been able to adapt fairly well to the representative institutions and the bureaucracy that were grafted onto traditional authority structures. In former French colonies, by contrast, traditional authority structures have been destroyed and replaced. In these countries bureaucracies are now more corrupt and political processes tend to be more authoritarian in nature.[26]

The impact of the political diffusion of ideas of representation has varied from one country to another. It frequently has been impossible to graft democratic political institutions onto societies with authoritarian political cultures.[27] The contemporary political system in West Germany was modeled after United States' experiences. But democratic political institutions are somewhat foreign to past German experience, and it is questionable whether democracy could be sustained in West Germany without continued economic prosperity. There are other cases where the imposition of authoritarian control has not been well-received in societies with at least semidemocratic political cultures. Most of Eastern Europe stagnated for two decades under an externally imposed Stalinist model of strict hierarchical political control unsuited to the developmental tasks and unrelated to historical experience in several of these countries.

Another important exogenous source of conflict is the colonial heritage itself. The boundaries of many new nations have been previously set by colonial powers. The boundaries existing at the time of independence often did not coincide with ethnic, tribal, cultural, or geographic divisions. As a result, many of the new nations are composed of a great diversity of tribes or ethnic groups having long histories of hatred and warfare among themselves. In Nigeria, for example, independence from Great Britain was granted in 1960, but in the absence of British authority the country quickly disintegrated into warring factions. In 1966 the Ibo tribe, which was dominant in Eastern Nigeria, engineered a military coup d'etat that ousted a previous civilian government. But the Hausa and Fulani tribes in the North and the Yoruba tribe in the West quickly took revenge. Ibos were massacred by the tens of thousands and their futile attempts to secede from Nigeria and create a new nation, Biafra, were overcome by military force. The Nigerian experience, creation of a state with little potential for becoming a nation, has been repeated in the Congo and many other former colonial territories in Africa.[28]

Another exogenous source of domestic conflict is economic in nature. The fragile economies of developing countries are highly dependent upon the industrial countries of the world for continued progress. Ruling political elites in these countries need economic progress to guarantee their continued tenure in office. Therefore they are vulnerable to sabotage, both intended and accidental, from the industrial world. Sometimes these disruptions have direct political intent, such as punitive withdrawal of economic aid. The socialist Allende government in Chile, for example, fell prey to political enemies in late 1973 when the United States withdrew both public and private economic aid and invested more than eight million dollars in expediting the downfall of the regime. Other domestic disruptions can result from investment decisions of large multinational corporations or simply from international economic trends. In 1973–74 many economic development programs received a severe setback from the rapidly spiraling price of crude oil, a factor over which political regimes in many less-developed countries had little control.

Endogenous Sources of Conflict. Political leaders in developing countries often use these exogenous sources of disruption as scapegoats to explain internal problems. Thus, the phrase "neocolonialism" is frequently employed to cover a multitude of economic and political failures. In reality, however, there are many endogenous sources of conflict within the elite circles of developing countries.

Opposition to colonial rule once unified indigenous political forces in many contemporary developing nations. But as anticolonialism lost some of its fervor and external colonial enemies began to disappear, new fissures appeared within modernizing political leadership. Many leaders have attempted to create new enemies to overcome internal cleavages while others such as Mao Tse-tung in China or Fidel Castro in Cuba have continued to wear revolutionary uniforms to keep revolutionary spirit alive.[29] In spite of these attempts, however, these leaders are often divided into factions and frequently there is internal disagreement on goals. Some politicians use their high office to retain traditional prerogatives or to destroy old opponents. Others are interested in developing a unified nation. Still other politicians are primarily interested in economic development at any cost. Finally, some hold democracy and political participation to be primary goals, even at the expense of instability and slower industrial development. Whatever the mix of contending points of view, ruling political elites in modernizing countries are often fragmented and are likely to lack common purpose in the absence of a colonial or "neocolonial" enemy.

A need for new enemies and drastic actions to heal open wounds can explain some apparent policy absurdities in developing countries. These include frequent charges of neoimperialism that are indiscriminately hurled against other nations, unthinking seizure of foreign economic assets, aggressive postures toward bordering nations, internal and external wars fought with religious fervor, and mass expulsions of minority groups such as that carried out against Indians and other Asians by Idi Amin (Big

Daddy) Dada in Uganda in 1973. A need for simple explanations and ideologies where divisiveness is common also helps explain the appeal of communism and authoritarian models of leadership.

Lack of consensus among rulers also helps to explain a heavy military presence in developmental politics. Military intervention has recurred in the form of coups and countercoups "in most Latin American republics, in five independent Arab states, in fourteen new African states, in several Southeast Asian polities, and in Pakistan."[30] It is not that the military frequently conspires to take power, but the military serves as a major source of stability when power struggles develop. Although military officers are also often divided on policy issues, the military is frequently the most cohesive, professional, and modernizing force in such situations. Military officers share many values in common and are usually united by a desire to maintain stability and insure economic progress. Huntington sees what he calls "praetorian" politics in less-developed countries as resulting from the political and social structures in such societies.[31] Perlmutter has identified a list of factors that contribute to praetorianism including a low degree of social cohesion, existence of fratricidal classes, social polarity, lack of a middle class, weak and ineffective political parties, a low level of political institutionalization, and persistent differences between centralizing and peripheral leaders.[32]

Political authority in developing nations is also endangered by corruption and political leadership based on primordial loyalties. Traditional ties to family, caste, tribes, etc. impede formation of the more generalized interest groups that are essential to the development of political stability. A politics of localism promotes distrust of national political leaders, disrespect for new political institutions, and prevents the transfer of loyalties necessary for nation-building. Unless people identify themselves as citizens of the larger nation rather than as members of tribes, castes, or kin groups, a national politics and public interest cannot develop and political community cannot be built.

Corruption flourishes in many less-developed countries and can be particularly harmful. Scott has pointed out that political machines prosper under conditions where many voters cast off traditional ties but do not develop strong occupational or new class ties. He documents substantial political corruption associated with modernizing parties in both Ghana and India.[33] Rewarding members of family, tribe, caste, or party through appointments or through government contracts is common practice, one that often leads to waste and inefficiency. Where politics is of a communal type and where it is not clearly separated from social and political relations, the merits of policies are seldom debated and many policy decisions are made strictly along communal lines. This, of course, results in political instability and less than optimal public policy.

There are many other endogenous elite characteristics in developing countries that chip away at established authority and foster political instability. Political parties in these countries often come to represent a world view and total way of life for their members, a substitute for lost community. Parties, such as the Congress Party in India or the Communist Party in the People's Republic of China, tend to become all-embracing social movements. They are often built around the thought of one man (Nehru in India, Mao in China, Nkrumah in Ghana) and, when he dies, political unity dissipates and conflict over succession begins. Opposition parties or elites become labeled as enemies of the state or "counterrevolutionaries." Peaceful elections and voluntary surrender of office become unlikely as officials thus removed are likely to be shot as traitors. Responsible opposition parties are unknown in many developing nations since the dominant party preempts the field by identifying its future with the future of the country. This restricts the dimensions of political debate, retards the entry of new ideas and recruitment of new personnel into decision-making, hardens minority opposition to the political system, and fosters conspiracies since there is little opportunity to voice opposition legitimately.[34]

Finally, many endogenous factors that normally preserve stability by narrowing the variety and intensity of political demands are not found in less-developed countries. There are few established political traditions and there is little leadership consensus on the proper ends and means of politics. Incumbents and opposition often operate without benefit of well-understood rules. To this must be added the fact that new participants are often recruited into politics and dominant political parties at a very high rate. This politicization of life in the absence of established rules, values, and traditions aggravates problems of conflict management. Furthermore, since political participation tends to be of an affective or expressive nature, rationality often disappears and this compounds existing turmoil and violence.

Turning from elites to masses, scholars have found another almost endless list of endogenous causes of conflict in less-developed countries.³⁵ Many of these are related to the psychological traumas accompanying modernization which have been mentioned above. But economic factors are also important. A rapidly growing economy can be a great political asset because it increases regime remunerative power and indirectly helps build legitimacy. Poor economic performance, on the other hand, can trigger political instability. Authority is weakened and conflict fomented when increased productivity cannot keep up with a revolution of rising expectations. The migration of hundreds of thousands of individuals from traditional villages to urban areas is accompanied by growing material expectations. These migrants often expect political leaders to produce miracles in feeding and housing newly urbanized peasants.

The relationship between relative deprivation and social and political violence is a peculiar one. The level of *absolute deprivation* in a country has been found not to be directly related to social turmoil or to violence directed against political actors. There is relatively little overt conflict in those countries that are not yet caught up in an industrial revolution regardless of the existing level of poverty and misery. Any violence that does take place is of a traditional nature, tribal warfare, etc. and is not centered around economic issues. It is only when something happens to cause expectations to rise that social and political violence and instability become more frequent.

Gurr has suggested that there are three different varieties of relative deprivation responsible for creating discontent.³⁶ *Decremental deprivation* occurs when collective value aspirations remain fairly constant over time but ruling political elite capabilities of meeting these expectations diminish. This can happen in industrial countries during periods of depression (many industrial nations in the 1930s), in developing countries when programs of industrial development experience setbacks (many developing countries during the petroleum crisis of 1973–74), or in agricultural countries when crops fail (India or Northern Africa in the 1970s). *Aspirational deprivation* occurs when value aspirations rise sharply while capabilities remain much the same. This is the type of relative deprivation that is most frequently found in less-developed countries. Rising expectations can quickly outrun the ability of ruling political elites to allocate limited resources. *Progressive deprivation* occurs when value aspirations rise for a time coincident with increasing capabilities, but aspirations then continue to rise as capabilities level off. This also occurs in developing countries as economic growth may at first keep up with rising expectations, but then can fall behind as economic problems become more complex.

Additional endogenous economic problems stem from huge income gaps that cause friction between the very rich and the very poor. There is also an almost total absence of any middle class in many developing countries. A large middle class seems essential to political stability and the development of democratic forms of government. Trade unions, farmers organizations, consumers groups, and civic organizations do not play independent political and economic roles similar to those that they play in industrial democracies. Instead, they become auxiliaries of a dominant party.[37]

Unemployment adds another dimension of economic conflict. Employment opportunities in developing countries frequently cannot meet rising job expectations. Often employment opportunities do not rise nearly as fast as the rate at which peasants leave the land. In some developing countries industry will never be able to create jobs for all those who migrate to the cities. In many of these developing countries there are hundreds of thousands of unemployed or underemployed persons available to form mobs at the slightest provocation. In addition, many young persons who receive college educations abroad cannot find "adequate" employment upon their return and they represent a reservoir of "alienated intellectuals" from which revolutionary leadership can be recruited.

Development or Decay?

There are few indications that civil strife in contemporary developing nations is diminishing. Since the end of World War II successful coups d'etat have occurred in eighteen of twenty Latin American countries. Turmoil, conspiracies, internal wars, and other types of violence have afflicted almost all newly emerging nations. The petroleum and related international monetary crises have exacerbated international problems of development. The forces of economic nationalism are again becoming extremely potent in the face of inflation and recession in the industrial world. This could signal a decline in international cooperation and mean additional trouble for developing countries.

Given these prospects it is questionable whether the traditional view that most of the Third World is developing economically and politically is a valid one. Perhaps there is a large fourth—or never-to-be-developed—world. De Schweinitz is pessimistic about the possibility that state-controlled economies will develop democratic political processes as did some of those nations that preceded them along the path to modernity.[38] Analysis of the sequences and time periods that were historically involved in the development of stability and democracy and comparisons with contemporary situations could also lead to pessimistic conclusions.[39]

Given this perspective, Huntington's concept of political development as a "relational" process in which development or decay can take place, depending upon the ability of ruling political elites to successfully manage "loads" placed upon decision-making systems, seems relevant. Political instability, according to Huntington, is due to lack of community.[40] Community results when there is a balanced relationship between demands of an ethnic, religious, economic, territorial, or social nature on one hand, and the capacity of political incumbents and institutions to absorb and satisfy them on the other. Where localist and separatist tendencies are few, and where class conflict and societal complexity are low, well-established or developed political institutions may not be necessary to preserve stability. In complex and modern societies strong, clearly defined and established political structures capable of exacting compliance from heterogeneous populations are necessary.

Huntington equates institutionalization with political development and defines political institutions as developed when they are adaptable, complex, autonomous, and coherent.[41] *Adaptability* in political institutions means a capability to adjust to new and different challenges. The older and more established an institution, the more likely it is to have developed a capacity for such response. First-generation revolutionary leaders are less likely to be as adaptable as the generations that follow. Later generations are likely to be more willing to compromise and to have different attitudes toward politics than those "present at the beginning." A political system's adaptability is also related to the variety of specific functions that it can perform. If maintaining order occupies all its resources, a political system may not be able to adapt to new challenges.

Complexity in political institutions means diversification of subunits within the system. If such diversification exists, conflict and citizen pressures can be effectively routed to many parts of the system. Should one part collapse, others are capable of taking up the slack. In the United States, for example, loss of a president through natural death or assassination, does not imperil the whole political process. Other parts of the political system take up the slack until a new president is able to take control. In many developing countries, however, loss of a charismatic political leader means a tremendous setback for political stability.

Autonomy of political institutions is also a facet of political development. In less-developed countries political institutions are not sharply differentiated from social institutions. While congruence among political and social values is essential to political stability, political institutions without autonomy often become captives of social groups. Thus, governments lacking autonomy are frequently the targets of coups d'etat, guerrilla movements, subversion, or other types of social interference with political processes. There is little room for compromise in situations where dedicated groups seek to capture politics for their own purposes and are unwilling to abide by constitutional principles because they "own" the government.

Finally, the more *unified* and *coherent* political leadership, the easier it is to deal with civil strife. When ruling elites are unified in the goals that they seek, they can much more effectively cope than when they are divided. In emerging nations anti-colonialism originally supplied some coherence, but as the enemy has faded in immediacy, political elites have often fallen to quarreling among themselves.

Huntington explains the persistence of violence and instability in less-developed countries, that is, political decay, to be the result of tremendous loads placed on these political systems that are not adaptable, complex, autonomous, and coherent. Political decay, however, is not limited to less-developed countries. Although the international energy crisis has had its most significant effect on economic development programs and indirectly on political stability in less industrial countries, the industrial world has not been immune. New problems and pressures coming from the international environment have created new loads and political decay in the industrial as well as the less industrial world. But the industrial world has more highly developed political institutions and can more easily cope with these new problems.

REFERENCES

1. One of the best collections of perspectives on modernization is M. Weiner, ed., *Modernization: The Dynamics of Growth*. New York: Basic Books, 1966.
2. K. Deutsch, "Social Mobilization and Political Development," *The American Political Science Review* (September 1961): 94–95.
3. See C. Geertz, "The Integrative Revolution: Primordial Sentiments and Civic Politics in the New States," in C. Geertz, ed., *Old Societies and New States: The Quest for Modernity in Asia and Africa*. New York: The Free Press, 1963.
4. D. Lerner, *The Passing of Traditional Society: Modernizing the Middle East*. New York: The Free Press, 1958, pp. 49ff.
5. A. Inkeles, "The Modernization of Man," in M. Weiner, ed., *Modernization: The Dynamics of Growth*. New York: Basic Books, 1966.
6. J. Kahl, *The Measurement of Modernism: A Study of Values in Brazil and Mexico*. Latin America Monographs, No. 12. Austin: University of Texas Press, 1968.
7. L. Doob, *Becoming More Civilized: A Psychological Exploration*. New Haven: Yale University Press, 1960, pp. 93–94, 149ff.
8. R. Clark, Jr., *Development and Instability: Political Change in the Non-Western World*. Hinsdale, Ill.: Dryden Press, 1974, pp. 32–34.
9. Clark, *Development and Instability: Political Change in the Non-Western World*, ch. 2.
10. For a more complete discussion of aspects of political development see G. Almond and G. Powell, *Comparative Politics: A Developmental Approach*. Boston: Little, Brown, 1966, pp. 34ff.
11. These relationships are treated in detail for empires in S. Eisenstadt, *The Political Systems of Empires*. New York: Free Press, 1962.
12. See R. Bendix, *Nation-Building and Citizenship: Studies of Our Changing Social Order*. New York: Wiley, 1964, pp. 33–48.
13. Almond and Powell, *Comparative Politics: A Developmental Approach*, p. 35.
14. Almond and Powell, *Comparative Politics: A Developmental Approach*, p. 36.
15. T. Marshall, *Sociology at the Crossroads*. London: Heinemann, 1963, ch. 4.
16. B. Moore, Jr., *Social Origins of Dictatorship and Democracy*. Boston: Beacon Press, 1966.
17. Moore, *Social Origins of Dictatorship and Democracy*.

18. Moore, *Social Origins of Dictatorship and Democracy*.
19. K. De Schweinitz, *Industrialization and Democracy*. New York: Free Press, 1963, chs. 9 and 10.
20. De Schweinitz, *Industrialization and Democracy*, p. 10.
21. De Schweinitz, *Industrialization and Democracy*, chs. 1 and 10; L. Binder et al., *Crises and Sequences in Political Development*. Princeton: Princeton University Press, 1971.
22. Clark, *Development and Instability: Political Change in the Non-Western World*.
23. F. Riggs, *Administration in Developing Countries: The Theory of Prismatic Society*. Boston: Houghton Mifflin, 1964, pp. 38–42.
24. H. Eckstein, "On the Etiology of Internal Wars," in I. Feierabend, R. Feierabend, T. Gurr, eds., *Anger, Violence, and Politics: Theories and Research*. Englewood Cliffs, N.J.: Prentice-Hall, 1972, p. 17.
25. E. Rogers and F. Shoemaker, *Communication of Innovations: A Cross-Cultural Approach*, 2d ed. New York: Free Press, 1971, pp. 14–18.
26. J. Coleman and C. Rosburg, Jr., "African One-Party States and Modernization," in C. Welch, ed., *Political Modernization*. Belmont, Calif.: Wadsworth, 1967.
27. Eckstein argues that political stability is likely if a nation has authority patterns congruent with the values of the society in which these patterns are found. See H. Eckstein, "A Theory of Stable Democracy," in Feierabend, Feierabend, and Gurr, *Anger, Violence, and Politics: Theories and Research*. For information about the peculiar case of German democracy see L. Edinger, *Politics in Germany*. Boston: Little, Brown, 1968, chs. 4 and 10.
28. Clark, *Development and Instability: Political Change in the Non-Western World*, pp. 170–76.
29. See R. Emerson, "The Problem of Identity, Selfhood, and Image in the New Nations," *Comparative Politics* (April 1969).
30. A. Perlmutter, "The Praetorian State and the Praetorian Army," *Comparative Politics* (April 1969): 382.
31. S. Huntington, *Political Order in Changing Societies*. New Haven: Yale University Press, 1968, ch. 4.
32. Perlmutter, "The Praetorian State and the Praetorian Army."
33. J. Scott, *Comparative Political Corruption*. Englewood Cliffs, N.J.: Prentice-Hall, 1972, ch. 8.
34. See L. Pye, *Politics, Personality, and Nation Building*. New Haven: Yale University Press, 1962, ch. 2.
35. For a summary of endogenous causes of conflict see Clark, *Development and Instability: Political Change in the Non-Western World*, ch. 6.
36. T. Gurr, *Why Men Rebel*. Princeton, N.J.: Princeton University Press, 1970, pp. 46–56.

37. See Perlmutter, "The Praetorian State and the Praetorian Army," pp. 385–91.
38. De Schweinitz, *Industrialization and Democracy*, pp. 273–279.
39. See Binder, et al., *Crises and Sequences in Political Development*, passim.
40. Huntington, *Political Order in Changing Societies*, pp. 8–11.
41. Huntington, *Political Order in Changing Societies*, pp. 12–24.

4
DEMOCRACY AS CONFLICT MANAGEMENT

The evolution of mass democracy as a method of making collective decisions has been a result of the industrial revolution. Prior to the advent of industrialization, experiments with democracy were few and they certainly were not experiments with mass democracy. Even the classic democracy of Ancient Greece was restricted to male citizens and citizenship was a privilege held by the wealthy few who ruled over others to whom it was denied.

Mass democracy has also emerged as a response to problems of conflict management. Industrialization historically has created new aspirations among previously disenfranchised groups. Ruling political elites have "purchased" social stability by expanding electorates. Co-opting dissident leaders into decision-making processes has proved to be an excellent method of diminishing potential revolutionary violence. The economic growth that accompanies industrialization has permitted ruling oligarchies to create and extend new resources and positions without endangering their own affluence. Growth has thus been an important factor responsible for the political stability and democracy that has accompanied industrialization.

Democratic rules of political competition represent a sophisticated method of dampening conflict. Since "the people" ostensibly play a critical role in collective decision-making through periodic elections, the election of poor leaders or the framing of poor public policies can be blamed on "the people," not on some self-perpetuating ruling political elite. Ruling political elites consider democracy to be a desirable method of conflict management because it is based upon voluntary citizen compliance. Citizens become more readily committed to collective goals that they perceive themselves as having played a role in formulating.[1] Citizen *perceptions* of themselves as playing a role in formulating collective policies is critical to democratic political stability. Democratic government is government by a *legitimate* oligarchy and legitimacy is as much a matter of perception as it is of empirical fact.

Democracy is a concept that is extremely difficult to define and measure. Intuitively everyone knows what it is. But perhaps because most people living in democracies have internalized the values, rhetoric, and myths of democracy it is difficult to understand it adequately. The United States and Great Britain are countries in which people consider democracy to be practiced. The Soviet Union and the People's Republic of China are usually not understood to be democracies. But when attempts are made to specify measurement rules by which a comparative determination of levels of democracy can be made, a number of serious problems arise.[2] Using election statistics as a criterion can be misleading, particularly since a greater percentage of voters turns out for elections in the Soviet Union than in Great Britain or in the United States! Similar problems arise if the number of competing political parties is used as an index of democracy. Is political competition in Yugoslavia really less democratic than the pseudo-competition between Republicans and Democrats in the United States or between the Conservative and Labor parties in Great Britain?

Robert Dahl has attempted to cope with this definitional problem by compiling a list of eight guarantees that he feels are necessary for democracy to work. These relate to citizen ability to formulate preferences, effectively to signify these preferences, and to the possibility of having these preferences weighted equally in the conduct of government. Among his guarantees are freedom of expression, freedom to form and join organizations, the right to vote, free elections, alternative sources of information, etc. Dahl concludes that there are no true democracies and he substitutes the term *polyarchy* to describe what people conventionally think of as democracy.[3]

Gregg and Banks have proceeded in a different manner. Using sophisticated factor analysis techniques and a pool of data available from the universe of nation-states, they have empirically isolated a concept called access, a group of variables that seem closely related to conventional definitions of democracy. Variables that cluster on this access dimension include type of electoral system, freedom of group opposition, press freedom, representativeness of regimes, and character of bureaucracy.[4]

Definitional problems aside, there are many factors that make democracy, as it is understood, a preferred method of conflict management. The most obvious is that citizens who have an opportunity to express policy preferences meaningfully during periodic elections are less inclined to violence than if such opportunities do not exist. Citizens also are likely to develop strong loyalties to political systems that they perceive to be responsive to their wishes. Coercion need not be used frequently when citizens feel that they play a key role in collective decision-making.

Democratic elections are also a political safety valve giving potential groups and new issues an opportunity to surface. Elections are a way of diminishing potentially destructive conflict through the competition that is reflected in electoral activity. Although elections are not necessarily peaceful (sometimes dozens or hundreds of persons are killed in elections in unstable democracies) the number of violent incidents associated with elections is only a fraction of those that could take place if there were no elections. The fact that periodic elections do take place in democracies means that frustrated losers in one election can look forward to attempting an upset of ruling majorities in the next election. As long as there is a general commitment to play by democratic rules, defeats at the ballot box are not likely to precipitate coups d'etat and other forms of intra-elite conflict.

DEMOCRATIC COMPETITION: MYTHS AND REALITY

There are two different types of factors that make democracy work. The first is psychological in nature and is rooted in the minds of citizens. These so-called myths of democracy form the psychological underpinnings of democratic political cultures. Citizens living in democracies believe them to be good systems for making decisions, believe that they personally play a role in making collective decisions, and perceive their political leaders to be responsive to their demands. They need not and often do not have a sophisticated empirical picture of how democratic systems actually work. The more empirical factors underlying democracies have been the subject of much scholarly study, and the literature that has resulted from these efforts is voluminous. The propositions that follow compare some of the psychological myths of democracy with what scholars have found to be the empirical world.

Citizens believe that they are political equals, particularly when it comes to electing and communicating with public officials. Empirically, however, some individuals are known to be much more influential in democratic politics than others. Wealth, for example, is a particularly important filtering device in selection of candidates for office as well as in influencing the outcome of elections. Many have made a cogent case that democratic ruling political elites are selected by monied power elites that successfully control political affairs.[5] Some have even argued that such power elites are essential to the persistence of democracies since the masses, if left to their own devices, would soon destroy the freedoms that they rhetorically hold to be so dear.[6] Stouffer, for example, has found that lower socioeconomic classes are much less likely to support civil liberties than are those of higher status.[7] Lipset has found that the lower strata in societies are much more likely to be "authoritarian" (willing to accept orders unquestioningly from the top) than are the upper strata.[8]

As paradoxical as it may seem, one of the essential empirical findings about mass democracy, indeed, one of the reasons that it works, is that a large proportion of the members of democratic publics do not have strongly held political opinions, do not participate actively in politics, and do not vote. Democracy persists partly because of "silent majorities," economically and politically satisfied people who have neither the time nor ambition to take an active role in politics. If all citizens held opinions very strongly and if all of them chose to become actively involved in politics, political chaos would be a likely result because satisfying most active participants would be extremely difficult. Silent majorities, therefore, help keep political struggles manageable and they diminish the potential alienation or bitterness that could result from hyperactive citizens pursuing many different policy alternatives with great passion.

Another factor known to be empirically helpful to the persistence of mass democracy is pluralism: competition among organized groups. While psychologically each individual thinks he or she has an important input into democratic political processes, those who are members of organized groups have a much stronger voice. Pluralist democracy depends upon the existence of a number of competing groups, each of which represents an independent locus of political power. Theorists of pluralist democracy claim that open competition and bargaining among organized groups ensures a free competition of ideas. When any group in a pluralist system attempts to seize total power its ambitions are soon checked by coalitions of the others. A pluralist system is thus self-correcting and democracy is maintained through a competition of groups, each seeking to protect its own interests.[9]

Schattschneider has corrected some of the naive pluralist notions of democracy by pointing out that the bias in pressure group politics is toward those of high socioeconomic status. Interests are not equally represented in pressure politics since the wealthy organize and join pressure groups much more frequently than do the poor. The whole system is skewed in favor of a small fraction of a minority. "If everybody got into the act the unique advantages of this form of organization would be destroyed, for it is possible that if all interests could be mobilized the result would be a stalemate."[10] The pluralism that preserves democracy is a pluralism within a controlling oligarchy. It is certainly not a system equally encompassing the interests of all the people.

Charles Lindblom has taken pluralist thinking one step further by claiming that the "intelligence of democracy" is found in the fact that in democratic systems "people can coordinate with each other without anyone coordinating them."[11] Lindblom uses economic analogies to demonstrate that stability is maintained in democracies because actors and groups take the preferences and actions of other groups into consideration when making their own decisions. When information is freely available in pluralist systems, *partisan mutual adjustment* represents a rational method of collectively "muddling through" without generating irreconcilable conflicts.[12] But partisan mutual adjustment only works well in environments of relative abundance where all involved groups *are willing* to take the preferences and actions of others into account.

Other empirical studies of democracy and stability have stressed the importance of *citizen membership in many groups* and *cross-cutting cleavages*. The importance of intermediary groups between citizen and political regimes has been stressed by Kornhauser as being essential to the preservation of political stability.[13] Individuals join many groups and develop multiple loyalties to them as part of the structural differentiation that accompanies industrialization.

There are three ways that the cross-cutting cleavage concept has been used to relate group membership and political phenomena. *Cross-pressures,* a closely related term used in the voting behavior literature, occur when individuals are members of many different groups, each group having different perspectives. Individuals must choose from these competing perspectives in making electoral choices. The dynamics involved in resolving these conflicting preferences have been used to explain various patterns of voting behavior.[14] There is also an extensive literature that concentrates on cross-cutting cleavages as regulators of social conflict. The real interdependence of supposedly antagonistic groups, their mutual interest in playing by a set of agreed-upon rules, and the overlapping of various perspectives and cleavages among them serve to sew the fabric of society together by canceling out much of the partisan fervor that could accumulate if cleavages were mutually reinforcing.[15] Cross-cutting cleavages in political parties are also understood to be essential for the preservation of a stable democracy.[16] Stability requires that major political parties include supporters from many different segments of society. When the support base for major political parties corresponds too closely with deep social cleavages, political stability and democracy are endangered by ideological fervor that can result.[17]

Political parties themselves are essential to democratic stability. Parties are the vehicle by which the many interests articulated by various individuals and groups are aggregated into policy packages, often expressed in political party platforms. Without political parties combining preferences into coherent programs, democracies could degenerate into anomic violence. Thus, although the conflict-diminishing role of parties is often overlooked, they do play an important role in reducing conflict and narrowing alternatives. It remains an open question, however, whether democracy requires competing political parties or whether democracy can be practiced in basically single-party regimes such as those in Mexico and Yugoslavia.

Finally, the empirical relationship between affluence and democracy should again be emphasized in explaining the existence of democracy. While myths ascribe a great deal of credit to the "democratic citizen," who is altruistic, concerned, and politically active, most individuals are more *economic* than *political*. It is much easier to maintain democratic rules of competition and avoid conflict under conditions of affluence than it is when economic problems restrict resources available for distribution. In fact, there is a reciprocal beneficial relationship between democracy and affluence: democratic political processes receive much of the credit in the public mind for creating economic affluence while affluence creates conditions conducive to democracy. This economic link is especially obvious in countries like West Germany where commitment to democracy has been tenuous. In West Germany democratic forms have been grafted onto a basically authoritarian political culture. A good argument can be made that West German democracy has been maintained only because of German economic prosperity.[18] As long as affluence continues democratic rules are likely to be praised and followed. It remains to be seen whether West Germany or other contemporary democracies can politically endure periods of economic depression and hardship.

LOCI OF COMPETITION

The myths of democracy portray political competition as taking place on the floors of legislatures where wise statesmen deliver impassioned speeches on the issues of the day before hundreds of their colleagues who listen with great interest. Open-minded legislators supposedly consider the issues, are influenced by rational arguments and debate, and then vote on the basis of the evidence presented. This is the culmination of the electoral process, chosen representatives of the people expressing constituents' preferences in decisions openly arrived at. But here too the rhetorical and empirical worlds differ greatly as the mythical and actual loci of political competition vary considerably.

Visitors to the United States Congress are shocked when they discover that their congressmen often make speeches to nearly empty chambers. Most senators and representatives visit the Senate or House floor only occasionally. In fact, many miss a substantial number of votes that are taken. The reason is that only a small portion of political competition actually takes place during legislative sessions. Major policy decisions are made elsewhere in both the United States and Great Britain and floor votes simply represent ratification of legislative packages that have been put together behind the scenes. In the United States Congress these packages are initially put together by party campaign platform committees, in caucuses, or in meetings of committees and subcommittees. In the British House of Commons legislative packages are decided by caucuses within the hierarchy of the governing party. It is only rarely that a government-sponsored bill is defeated on the floor of the House of Commons. When this does happen, it almost always precipitates a governmental crisis and new elections.

The debates in both the British House of Commons and the

United States Congress are, to a great extent, propaganda aimed at mollifying constituents and at preparing for the next election. In Congress much of the fiery rhetoric bears no relation to final votes on important pieces of legislation. Many senators and representatives publicly ranted and railed at the oil industry for price gouging and excessive profits during the energy crisis of 1973–74. But when many of those who had protested most loudly against the actions of oil companies voted on energy issues, the record showed a gap between their public speeches and actual voting behavior. Even roll-call tabulations are often misleading as many senators and representatives vote against their own convictions on bills when the fate of the bill is already decided. This permits them to misrepresent their positions to their constituents, when necessary, and to prepare for the next election. Furthermore, many really important votes have been taken in closed committee sessions or are disguised as procedural matters or amendments.

Political campaigns represent one important locus of democratic competition. Party platforms, statements of political party policy, are hammered together before major electoral campaigns and planks of these platforms are frequently enacted into law by victorious parties. The hearings that accompany platform writing offer an opportunity for various interests to make their views known. Election campaigns themselves offer interest groups an opportunity to enter directly the competition for office.

But campaigns are costly affairs and money plays a key and anti-democratic role in determining the rules of competition. Recent presidential elections in the United States have cost the top candidates as much as sixty million dollars. It is estimated that over one-half billion dollars total was spent by all political candidates in the 1972 elections.[19] Candidates for office need money to be elected and this gives wealthy interests an opportunity to use economic pressures to exact legislative promises. Thus, in the presidential election of 1972 the oil industry, milk producers, weapons manufacturers, and various other business interests made large contributions to the Nixon campaign apparently seeking promises of favorable treatment. Many times political trade-offs are not so overt and campaign donations are often made in the interest of "good-will," "friendship," or purchasing "access" whenever it might be needed.

Lobbying activity is another focus of competition. Lobbyists representing various interests operate best within the Congressional Committee structure in the United States Congress and function more overtly as sources of expertise within the British bureaucracy. In the United States they operate by wining and dining, as well as occasionally cajoling, small groups of senators and representatives who represent the key votes in committees or subcommittees. Most politicians do not find this form of the competition of ideas to be inimical to the democratic process in spite of the sums of money involved. In fact, many find lobbyists to be a valuable source of information.

There are many other loci of political competition or even conflict within the United States government; mainly within the executive branch, the judiciary, and in regulatory agencies. Even though a bill may be enacted into law by Congress, for example, the executive branch makes its own decisions about the vigor with which the law will be enforced. And in terms of competition this can be every bit as important to the average citizen as the legislative process. Income tax laws, for example, would soon have little meaning if the Internal Revenue Service consistently failed to audit returns. Civil rights legislation would also be almost meaningless if the power of the executive branch were not dedicated to enforcement.

A similar situation exists within regulatory agencies such as the Federal Communications Commission, the Securities and Exchange Commission, or the Federal Trade Commission. Although broad mandates for these agencies have been sketched out by Congress, their day-to-day decision-making represents another point at which various competitors make their pressure felt. In fact, cogent arguments have been made that regulatory agencies are regularly captured by the interests that they are supposed to regulate.[20]

Finally, although much less receptive to outside pressures, the judiciary also represents a point at which competitors can influence policy. Much competition is carried out in the guise of extended litigation dealing with interpretations of laws that have been passed by Congress. Money also plays a very important role in legal competition as only the wealthy can afford to retain attorneys and carry on protracted legal battles. The importance of the courts as a locus of competition and conflict is reflected in the extent to which defendants are increasingly "buying time" through costly appeals. In 1950, 2,830 cases were initiated in the United States Court of Appeals. In 1971, 12,788 cases were initiated.[21] Thus, while money is not frequently used to directly "buy" judges in the United States, it is important in outlining the shape of the judicial battleground. It determines what types of disputes are adjudicated at what levels and which groups get better treatment in the court system by virtue of their ability to retain superior counsel.

A United States Federal Trade Commission attempt to institute a program requiring disclosure of sensitive data by large business firms offers a good case study of how competition shifts from one locus to another within democratic political systems. In 1973 the Federal Trade Commission (FTC), which is charged with responsibility for enforcing anti-trust legislation and insuring business competition, attempted to institute a Line of Business Reporting Program that would require large corporations to report previously secret data dealing with profits and sales of various categories of items produced. Under the program corporations would be required to report profitability by product line, as well as domestic and foreign sales and profits, on the theory that this would help identify noncompetitive and overly profitable areas of commercial activity. Large corporations were obviously not enamored with these new regulations hatched by an administrative agency originally created by an act of Congress. Business interests felt that the regulations represented a major policy shift and that they should be debated in Congress where corporate promises, threats, and pressures could better determine the outcome.

Corporate forces made an initial attempt to stop the new FTC program through the president's Office of Management and Budget, which had the power to halt government requests for data when these requests duplicate other surveys or put too much burden on those being studied. Interested business executives reasoned that since the head of the Office of Management and Budget was Roy Ash, a former business executive himself, his office would intervene to overrule the FTC plan. But this corporate maneuver was blunted by a legislative amendment to a bill authorizing construction of the Alaskan oil pipeline. A group of liberal senators saw the pipeline bill as an opportunity to attach a "rider" to counter the corporate thrust into the Office of Management and Budget. The amendment to the pipeline bill trimmed the Office of Management and Budget's power to oversee government requests for data and transferred this power to the General Accounting Office, which is under congressional control.

Having lost this initial skirmish in Congress, business lobbyists then turned their attention to other pressure points. The next in line was the president. Although a Republican president was certainly sympathetic to their pleas, indeed corporate executives had made hundreds of thousands of dollars of illegal contributions to his 1972 campaign, he declined their request to veto the pipeline bill. To do so would have jeopardized the Alaskan pipeline, a goal for which the administration had fought for several years. The chief executive signed the bill and the attached rider which transferred blocking authority over the FTC program from the executive to the legislative branch.

Business lobbyists redoubled their behind-the-scenes efforts. Numerous business groups descended on the General Accounting Office to makes pleas to the agency to cut the FTC program. When it became known that the General Accounting Office would need expert help to deal with program operations, business lobbyists brought forward the names of several economists known to have a probusiness bias. Some of them were hired. Consumer groups countered by offering several economists known to be sympathetic to the FTC program. Three of them were then retained by the General Accounting Office as consultants. Business forces then approached conservative Jamie Whitten of Mississippi, Chairman of the House Agricultural Appropriations Subcommittee, which, ironically, has jurisdiction over FTC funding. Their hope was to get the Whitten committee to cut off funds for the controversial program. In addition, business leaders expressed willingness to use financial and legal muscle in the courts, contesting the FTC program on constitutional grounds.

In summary, the FTC Line of Business Reporting Program represents a good example of how the locus of political competition can shift from official legislatures to various other pressure points within democratic political systems. Millions of dollars are spent annually in the United States by lobbyists attempting to buy, threaten, or convince officials in sensitive positions of the merits of their causes. The great number of points at which time and money can be mobilized to maintain pressures against change frustrates many policy initiatives. The fact that money is more generally available to those who oppose new causes is one of the reasons that rapid social and political change is very difficult in mass democracies. This is considered a virtue of democracy by those who seek to preserve traditions and a vice by radicals who desire rapid change.

Nondecisions and Stability

In democracies, issues and preferences must be brought to collective attention in order for them to be translated into public policy. While this may seem obvious enough, it is not so obvious that only a small fraction of all *potential* issues ever gets publicly debated. There is a large area of consensus in all societies. This consensus is created by customs, norms, beliefs, and values that most people accept. Many potential issues are hidden within it and are never called to public attention. Constitutions explicitly spell out many of these fundamental beliefs and principles which are subject to question only in times of stress and revolution. But apparent consensus is also created through political activity. Political leaders seek to narrow political debate by using conflict management resources to prevent many potential political issues from receiving public exposure. Thus, in every stable political system there is a very large number of what Bachrach and Baratz call "nondecisions," issues that never get openly debated, but that could be every bit as important to collective welfare as the issues that are openly discussed.[22]

Consensus is a very complex concept. It is closely related to nondecisions and its nature and extent vary among political systems. Spiro has suggested that consensus on some common goals is a prerequisite for political community while dissensus on methods and procedures is essential for politics. Politics begins only when consensus breaks down. "A political system is a community processing its issues."[23] Downs has made a distinction between a *consensus of intensities* and a *consensus of views*. In stable communities most citizens agree upon the issue areas that are most important (intensities) while they do not necessarily agree on which policies to follow on any particular issue (views).[24]

While it may seem a bit of a paradox, political competition often takes place through suppression of issues that may produce conflict.[25] In all political systems well-organized interests maintain social stability and their traditional prerogatives by keeping new issues from public attention. There are two aspects of government by nondecision. One involves conscious agreements within a ruling oligarchy to keep certain issues out of politics. Many issues become public only "because someone wants to make certain that the power ratio among the private interests most immediately involved shall not prevail."[26] But many other potential issues remain nondecisions because of apathy among those in a position to activate them. Regardless of the reasons that these many "nonissues" remain submerged, it is a fact that well-organized and wealthy interests are normally much more concerned with "law and order," "stability," "minimal government," etc., while the poor and minorities seek to break what they consider to be an oppressive status quo and bring previously submerged issues into the open.

It is extremely rare that individuals can break these conspiracies of silence and turn these nondecisions into political issues. Either such potential issues must find a tremendous amount of support among others who are similarly affected or they must be championed by political influentials who act as issue brokers. This is closely related to controversies in democracies over fairness of the mass media. Control of the mass media is essential to issue management. An issue raised on a television news program or a story printed on the front page of a newspaper reaches millions of people. Thus, when the media seizes upon a nonissue it can easily make it into an issue because of the tremendous multiplier effect inherent in mass media exposure. It is not necessary that media personnel deliberately suppress issues. Benign neglect works as well. The Nixon administration attacks on press credibility in the United States can be easily understood from this perspective. Without the media playing an active role in revealing facts about the Watergate affair and associated campaign abuses, they would have remained secret and thereby would have been nonissues.

The scope of legitimate government action varies considerably among nations. Scope is related to the decision-nondecision distinction and refers to the number of policy areas within which government policy-making is tolerated. In the United States, for example, a tradition of limited government was enshrined in the constitution and this tradition has persisted. Those who attended the Constitutional Convention were predominantly large landowners and men of commerce. Their primary fear, a reaction to the monopolies that had been established by the British Crown, was of a strong central government that would interfere with free enterprise and related economic freedoms. They quite understandably established a weak central government and restricted its scope to necessary activities such as coining money, providing for a common defense, and facilitating interstate commerce.[27] In

Great Britain, the Scandinavian countries, and in some continental European countries the scope of government power is much larger and includes government operation of essential industries, national health care, guaranteed income levels, etc.

A narrow definition of the scope of legitimate government action also means that many issues around which political conflict might center remain nondecisions. Many potential issue areas that remain in the private sector have a great impact on the collective quality of life. Throughout United States history, for example, private decisions by private corporations to dump waste products into lakes and streams or to discharge pollutants into the atmosphere have had a large impact on those living downstream or downwind. It was not until the passage of the National Environmental Protection Act in 1969 that the scope of government power was enlarged to encompass these previous nondecisions related to the preservation of environmental integrity. At present, Congress, the Environmental Protection Agency, and the courts are deeply involved in passing and enforcing legislation designed to prevent environmental abuse and to force private corporations to internalize the environmental costs of their operations. There are many other policy areas in which private decisions that have detracted from collective welfare in the past will undoubtedly fall before an increasing scope of government control in the near future.

Economic issues are very important to collective welfare and many of them are now settled outside of political processes in the United States. Although the president of the United States has a Council of Economic Advisors, a Federal Reserve System, and monetary and fiscal tools at his command, private economic interests are capable of subverting public policies in this area. Inflation policy offers a good example. If the nation's large steel manufacturers raise prices by ten percent across the board, this action could have the same inflationary impact on the economy as a decision by the Federal Reserve Board to loosen credit. Similarly, if the United Mine Workers or the United Steelworkers exact big salary increases through collective bargaining, there could also be serious inflationary repercussions throughout society. In Great Britain, by contrast, public ownership of mines means that mine workers' salaries are a political issue settled by political competition or conflict.

In summary, conflict can be avoided in democratic political systems by consciously burying potential conflicts or ignoring them (nondecisions) or by keeping responsibility for certain types of decision-making in the private sector (restricted scope). The larger the scope of government activity, the greater the *potential* responsiveness of collective institutions to the will of the politically active segment of the population and the greater the range of nondecisions that become political issues. The larger the scope of government control the more likely it is that political leaders will be held responsible for policy failures. On the other hand, political leaders are also likely to get greater credit for successful policies.

Unresolved Tensions in Democracies

One of the great strengths of democracy lies in the appeal of its myths for individual citizens. Theory and rhetoric stress political equality, each person having an equal vote and voice in making collective decisions. The subtle flattery of democracy has provided the impetus for its global spread as an ideal, if not a reality. But the popularity of democratic myths has often distracted attention from empirical analysis of its conflict management aspects as well as of the tensions that are hidden within it. There are many tensions between democratic rhetoric and democracy as an efficient managerial tool and way of reaching collective decisions.

There is an enduring tension between *democratic representation as a conflict management device and the need to elect "uncommon" men possessing expertise and wisdom to political office*. One of the sources of democratic stability is that citizens can elect people to political office with whom they can easily identify. This preserves a feeling of political efficacy and makes it appear that political leaders are really representative of the masses. Democratic political systems are optimal conflict management systems to the extent that social backgrounds of ruling political elites approximate those of constituents, to the extent that leaders and followers share value and issue perspectives, and to the extent that both agree on the role of the democratic representative.[28]

From the perspective of efficiency such a system of representation can only work well, however, when citizens are well-informed and elect well-informed individuals to office. When elected officials are similar to the masses they may adequately represent the electorate, but they are not necessarily uncommon men. The literate as well as the illiterate, the sober as well as the intoxicated, and the selfless as well as the selfish, all cast votes in democratic elections. A study of the United States electorate (1974) revealed the level of voter sophistication and understanding of social and political institutions to be very low. Twenty-four percent of all adults between the ages of 26 and 35 interviewed thought that presidential candidates are nominated by a national primary. The study also found that less than half of those interviewed knew how to use a paper ballot correctly and a substantial portion had reservations about applying basic constitutional guarantees to everyday situations.[29] While the myths of democracy ascribe to the average voter a certain mysterious ability to pick the most qualified person for office, the historical record is spotty, at best.

The problems with which ruling political elites now must contend are much more complex than they have been in the past and often there are no simple answers. Making intelligent public policies for complex industrial societies requires marshaling functional expertise on a scale heretofore unknown in politics. An increasingly important tension will continue to exist between a growing need for educated, intelligent, sophisticated, and aware political elites and the conflict management aspect of democracy which stresses the representation of common folks by common folks.

A second tension persists in democracies between the *virtues of pluralism as a stability-inducing mechanism and the realities of political oligopoly*. The persistence of pluralist democracy depends upon self-correcting political mechanisms analogous to Adam Smith's invisible hand in economics. Defenders of pluralism assume that a wide variety of competitive interests will preserve democracy (or polyarchy), that cross-cutting cleavages will continue to prevent extremism, and that willingness to compromise and cooperate will preserve presently accepted democratic rules of competition. But politics in industrial societies, like economics, is increasingly characterized by oligopoly, a few large groups representing big concentrations of economic and political power. These powerful interests may not continue to play by the democratic rules of competition if it does not appear to be in their interest to do so. Lowi has pointed out that politics in the United States is increasingly characterized by rigidity and unwillingness of powerful groups to compromise.[30] While the theoretical ideas behind pluralism as a method of managing political conflict and preserving democracy are obvious, socioeconomic realities in complex mass societies continue to chip away at traditional bases for consensus and compromise.

A third conflict exists between the myth that *"the people" control in a democracy and the empirical studies that emphasize the key role played by strategic elites in managing democratic stability.* Keller has argued that structural differentiation in industrial societies has led to proliferation and partial autonomy of what she calls strategic elites. The variegated composition of and differing perspectives within this strategic elite preserve democracy and restrict possibilities for an all powerful oligarchy becoming a monolithic controlling force.[31] Truman has similarly argued that the stability and survival of democratic political systems depend upon a continuing consensus among ruling elites since they are more privileged and thereby have a special stake in system stability.[32]

The question of who *actually* rules in existing democratic political systems is a difficult and largely unanswered one. It is clear, however, that the individual voter plays a very limited role. C. Wright Mills coined the term "power elite" in the mid-1950s to describe an elite group that he considered to be the real source of power in the United States. According to Mills, a "rationalization" (differentiation) process which includes the proliferation of new technologies, large bureaucracies, and new techniques for manipulation of the public is taking place in all industrial societies. As a result of this trend power is becoming increasingly centralized in the hands of a small group of technocrat-politicians and this select group effectively rules quite apart from the formal trappings of democracy. According to Mills, membership in this interlocking elite directorate is made up of the corporate rich, a ruling political caste, and a group of warlords associated with the Defense Department; in short, a military-industrial complex. Members of this ruling group control social, economic, and political processes both within the supposedly democratic political system as well as through their control of "nondecision-making."[33]

Mills' arguments have ignited a continuing debate over the extent to which a self-perpetuating power elite now controls in the United States and the extent to which it ought to control.[34] G. William Domhoff has sought to support Mills' thesis by outlining the composition of an "inbred" dominant social class. He links this dominant social class to an upper economic class composed of America's business leaders; this upper socioeconomic

Democracy as Conflict Management

conglomerate being tightly knit together by stock ownership, marriage, membership in exclusive clubs, education in exclusive private schools, overlapping membership on corporate boards of directors, etc. Domhoff concludes that this upper socioeconomic class is also a "governing" class "which owns a disproportionate amount of the country's wealth, receives a disproportionate amount of the country's yearly income, and contributes a disproportionate number of its members to positions of leadership."[35]

Domhoff did a time-consuming job in attempting to document the tie between wealth and power in the United States. He found, as have others, that money enables a power elite to strongly influence supposedly democratic processes, largely through the financing of political campaigns. Money purchases advertising in magazines and newspapers. It also buys exposure on the electronic media. Money is an important element in determining the success or failure of various political ideas in a supposedly free competition of ideas in democracies.

It should be obvious even to the most dedicated defender of democratic virtue that all democracies, including those in the United States and Great Britain, are subject to Michels Iron Law of Oligarchy. The exigencies of modern technology, the tremendous challenges of managing a complex industrial society, and the inherent inequalities in semicompetitive economic systems all combine to produce a ruling class that makes most decisions affecting collective welfare. The crucial questions involve the rules for recruitment to this oligarchy and the extent to which it is influenced by public pressures. *It is these rules by which an oligarchy is selected, replaced, and influenced* that distinguish democracies from other types of political systems.

A fourth tension exists between the *conflict management requirement for periodic elections and efficiency needs for long-term planning.* Periodic elections are essential to maintain political accountability. They cement citizen loyalties to political systems, give citizens a feeling of political efficacy, and represent important means of political communication. But, periodic elections also detract from long-term planning. In the United States representatives are elected for only two-year terms, presidents for four years, and senators for six years. Thus, planning takes place in two-year, four-year, and six-year cycles as reelection is always on the minds of politicians. While long-term planning is increasingly required to cope with the complicated problems of industrial democracies, it flies in the face of the short-term political perspectives that result from periodic elections.

Pluralist democracies work well as systems for maintaining stability but function poorly when new policies are needed. Democracies provide stability during "normal" times because they codify past social experience and wisdom as filtered through the voting public. But democracies do very poorly at anticipating future problems. Proponents of democracy often argue that only the wearer can tell when a shoe pinches. Democratic citizens knew when the "shoe was pinching" in the past, but they have little conception of policies that will be necessary to keep "shoes from pinching" in the future.

Finally, tension exists between the *myth of freely available information and efficiency needs for secrecy* in governmental processes. The arguments in favor of secrecy in government are many and are frequently stated. "Diplomatic relations can only be conducted under the cover of secrecy." "Defense matters simply cannot be open to public scrutiny." "Political leaders can only work effectively when they are adequately insulated from public pressures." Secrecy is also an excellent way to keep certain types of conflict from arising, but it strikes at the heart of the democratic process: the need to supply citizens with as much information as possible so that they can adequately evaluate the performance of their representatives and make informed electoral choices. In Great Britain the Official Secrets Act and in the United States the concept of executive privilege and the requirements of national security can easily be used to keep potentially damaging and embarrassing information from public attention.

REFERENCES

1. See A. Etzioni, *A Comparative Analysis of Complex Organizations.* New York: Free Press, 1961, pp. 127–30, 146–49, 152–87.
2. These problems are discussed in detail in D. Neubauer, "Some Conditions of Democracy," *The American Political Science Review* (December 1967).
3. R. Dahl, *Polyarchy: Participation and Opposition.* New Haven: Yale University Press, 1971, pp. 2–3.
4. P. Gregg and A. Banks, "Dimensions of Political Systems: A Factor Analysis of a Cross-Polity Survey," *The American Political Science Review* (September 1965).

5. C. W. Mills, *The Power Elite*. New York: Oxford University Press, 1956; G. Domhoff, *Who Rules America?* Englewood Cliffs, N.J.: Prentice-Hall, 1967. See also G. Domhoff and H. Ballard, eds., *C. Wright Mills and the Power Elite*. Boston: Beacon Press, 1968.
6. See P. Bachrach, *The Theory of Democratic Elitism: A Critique*. Boston: Little, Brown, 1967, ch. 4 and references cited therein.
7. This can be inferred from data presented in S. Stouffer, *Communism, Conformity, and Civil Liberties*. New York: Wiley, 1966, chs. 3 and 4.
8. S. M. Lipset, *Political Man: The Social Bases of Politics*. New York: Doubleday, 1960, ch. 4.
9. See D. Truman, *The Governmental Process*. New York: Knopf, 1951; A. Bentley, *The Process of Government*. Evanston, Ill.: Principia Press, 1935; C. Lindblom, *The Intelligence of Democracy: Decision-Making Through Mutual Adjustment*. New York: Free Press, 1965.
10. E. Schattschneider, *The Semi-Sovereign People: A Realist's View of Democracy in America*. New York: Holt, Rinehart & Winston, 1960, p. 35.
11. Lindblom, *The Intelligence of Democracy*, p. 3.
12. Lindblom, *The Intelligence of Democracy*, p. 3; C. Lindblom, "The Science of Muddling Through," *Public Administration Review* (Spring 1959).
13. W. Kornhauser, *The Politics of Mass Society*. New York: Free Press, 1959.
14. P. Lazarsfeld, B. Berelson, and H. Gaudet, *The People's Choice*. New York: Columbia University Press, 1944.
15. R. Dahl, *A Preface to Democratic Theory*. Chicago: University of Chicago Press, 1956, pp. 104–5.
16. Lipset, *Political Man*, ch. 2.
17. For an overview of the "cross-cutting" concept, see M. Taylor and D. Rae, "An Analysis of Cross-Cutting Between Political Cleavages," *Comparative Politics* (July 1969).
18. See L. Edinger, *Politics in Germany*. Boston: Little, Brown, 1968, ch. 4.
19. D. Pirages and P. Ehrlich, *Ark II: Social Response to Environmental Imperatives*. San Francisco: W. H. Freeman, 1974, p. 139.
20. See G. McConnell, *Private Power and American Democracy*. New York: Knopf, 1966, chs. 6 and 10; T. Lowi, *The End of Liberalism: Ideology, Policy, and the Crisis of Public Authority*. New York: Norton, 1969, ch. 4.
21. *Statistical Abstract of the United States, 1972*. Washington, D.C.: U.S. Department of Commerce, 1973, p. 155.
22. P. Bachrach and M. Baratz, "Decisions and Non-Decisions: An Analytical Framework," *The American Political Science Review* (September 1963).

23. H. Spiro, "Comparative Politics: A Comprehensive Approach," *The American Political Science Review* (September, 1962).
24. A. Downs, *An Economic Theory of Democracy*. New York: Harper and Row, 1957, pp. 66–68.
25. Bachrach and Baratz, "Decisions and Non-Decisions: An Analytical Framework."
26. Schattschneider, *The Semi-Sovereign People*, p. 38.
27. T. Dye and L. Ziegler, *The Irony of Democracy: An Uncommon Introduction to American Politics*. Belmont, Calif.: Wadsworth, 1970, ch. 2.
28. For more perspective on varying definitions of the role of the representative in democracies, see H. Pitkin, *The Concept of Representation*. Berkeley: University of California Press, 1967, chs. 4–7.
29. The study was carried out by the National Assessment of Educational Progress Program and financed by the U.S. Office of Education.
30. Lowi, *The End of Liberalism*.
31. S. Keller, *Beyond the Ruling Class: Strategic Elites in Modern Society*. New York: Random House, 1963, esp. chs. 4 and 5.
32. D. Truman, "The American System in Crisis," *Political Science Quarterly* (December 1959).
33. Mills, *The Power Elite*.
34. See Domhoff and Ballard, *C. Wright Mills and the Power Elite*.
35. Domhoff, *Who Rules America?*

5
CONFLICT MANAGEMENT UNDER SOCIALISM

The study of socialist (communist) politics received a great impetus during the cold war years following World War II because political processes within these countries were thought to be very different from those found in other political systems.* Many scholars were interested in possible counterrevolution, some of them secretly or even openly hoping that communist parties in the Soviet Union and Eastern Europe would be forced from power. Differences between politics in the Soviet Union and in other political systems were stressed and many similarities were ignored. However, the nature of political conflict and methods of conflict management in the Soviet Union and other socialist countries are not different from those in other nations, but because of historical peculiarities in the development of socialism, conflict management has been more obvious in these countries.

The Russian Revolution of 1917 occurred within the lifetimes of many Russians who are still alive. The Bolshevik revolution took place in a poverty-stricken, agrarian society that was disoriented by years of war and internal strife. Russia was a developing nation and Russian problems of economic and political development were similar to those facing the leaders of today's new nations: consolidating political authority and accumulating capital to develop an industrial infrastructure. Furthermore, much of the economic development that has boosted the Soviet Union to second place among the world's industrial powers was carried out in

* In common language countries ruled by communist parties are referred to as communist. This is technically incorrect since no leaders of these countries claim that they have finished building socialist societies and have moved on to communism, a higher stage of development. Throughout, the term socialist is used in reference to communist party states in keeping with what socialist leaders claim to be their political situations. This runs the risk of confusing these socialist (communist) countries with other socialist countries such as Sweden, but clear distinctions will be made when references are made to this latter group of countries, which could best be called socialist democracies.

spite of the terrible destruction of World War II. It is questionable that such achievements would have taken place in the absence of considerable use of force.[1]

When the Bolsheviks took power in 1917 they were faced with a staggering burden of political and economic problems. Russia was still technically at war, foreign troops occupied considerable sections of the country, the economy was drained and shattered by war and revolution, and support for the Bolsheviks was much less than overwhelming. Given these conditions it was obvious to the Bolshevik leadership that a tightly knit "dictatorship of the proletariat" was necessary to guarantee authority over a restive and depleted society. Thus Lenin declared in "The State and Revolution" that revolution means the proletariat destroys the administrative apparatus and the whole state machine and replaces it with *a new one made up of armed workers*. Once this armed proletarian oligarchy was established in the Soviet Union, however, it proved not only to be durable against external enemies, but it developed an enduring life of its own.

The resulting tightly knit hierarchical model of decision-making, within which a very few made decisions for the many, was reinforced by the triumph of Joseph Stalin within the Communist Party soon after the death of Lenin. It is debatable how much of Stalin's fanatic social mobilization effort was made necessary by the critical economic and political problems facing the Party and how much was simply the result of his own peculiar psychological problems. The facts are that, beginning in 1929, Stalin launched a program of bloody purges within the CPSU (Communist Party of the Soviet Union) and a collectivization effort in the Russian countryside that eventuated in terror and bloodshed throughout the Soviet Union.[2] By the time of his death in 1953 Stalin had created a one-man dictatorship that based its authority almost entirely upon terror and coercion, and he had exported this method of rule to the rest of the socialist bloc.

According to Marxist theory, once a socialist revolution could be accomplished, a transition to communism could begin. Ideally, under communism there would be no serious conflict as each person would contribute according to ability and take only according to needs. Thus, the coercive institutions of government and politics would "wither away." Needless to say, the transition to communism has been repeatedly delayed in the Soviet Union and other socialist countries and a "command" system of making decisions persists as an anomaly in many of these industrially de-

Conflict Management Under Socialism

veloped socialist societies. Not only have the state institutions not withered away, but the scope and pervasiveness of their power have become much greater than in many other industrial political systems.

Aside from the fact that the state was to wither away under communism, Karl Marx specified very little else about political authority in his communist utopia. Little was written about the transition to a society in which "new socialist men" would be willing to contribute according to ability and to take only according to need. Thus, the ways in which resources and positions would be authoritatively allocated under communism were not clearly specified in Marxist theory and this allocation has been largely determined by the revolutionary and wartime exigencies that have shaped and maintained a strong dictatorship of the proletariat in the Soviet Union.

It is therefore understandable that Lenin, Stalin, and the Bolshevik leadership opted for government by a small group of decision-makers well insulated from public pressure. A revolution, a worldwide depression, and World War II, in which Russia suffered tremendous loss of life, added to the pressures that helped to maintain a command mobilization model of political organization until Stalin's death in 1953.

Under Lenin and Stalin, Communist Party control became pervasive on all levels in Soviet society, and this pattern of tight control was reproduced, in time, throughout the socialist world. A high degree of centralization and strict discipline were important to the fledgling CPSU in maintaining its authority. These ideas found expression in the "doctrine of democratic centralism" which remains essential to CPSU discipline. The doctrine states that:

1. There should be election of all Party bodies from the lowest to the highest.
2. There should be periodic reports by Party bodies to the main Party organization and to higher bodies.
3. There should be strict Party discipline and subordination of the minority to the majority.
4. Decisions of higher level bodies are binding on lower bodies.

Democratic centralism theoretically means that free elections should be held for all Party offices and that open discussion of critical issues should be encouraged, at least until a higher body passes authoritatively on them. In reality, democratic centralism represents the theoretical basis for a political system in which free elections and democratic rules of competition have long been absent.

ACCESS AND LEGITIMACY

The Soviet hierarchical model of decision-making, with its restricted citizen access and limited opportunities for effective citizen participation, offered many managerial advantages during periods of intense industrialization and social mobilization. It now has great appeal for ruling political elites in less-developed nations where loads on political systems in the form of economic, social, and political demands are so great that they cannot be met within existing structures of political and economic opportunities.[3] Coercion and tight control from above are essential to "demand reduction" under these conditions and can be effectively used to maintain authority during periods of reconstruction or intensive economic development when pecuniary rewards cannot match citizen expectations. This Soviet command system of authority is at least partially responsible for the rapid Soviet recovery from the Civil War and two world wars and for the high level of industrialization that is found in the Soviet Union today. But the toll of human suffering and lost creativity that has resulted from this command system has also been very great. Economic advances have not always been sufficient to erase old hostilities and build the legitimacy that the present regime would like.

When a nation is being built in a highly fragmented society or when rapid industrialization of an agrarian economy is desired, decentralized authority can be disastrous and hierarchical decision-making backed by coercion is necessary. Sanctions are very effective in exacting performance from unskilled labor for little compensation.[4] Minimal citizen commitment is required during early stages of industrialization and it can be exacted through sanctions since heavy manual labor requires little sophistication or special ability. The Egyptian pyramids were apparently built largely with the persuasion of the whip just as much of Soviet heavy industry was built under the threat of starvation or other forms of torture.[5] As long as the work that must be done is easily quantified and requires minimal skill (mining coal or hauling concrete), coercion and withdrawal of privileges is enough to insure adequate performance.

Command decision-making loses effectiveness, however, when

initial mobilization-type tasks have been completed. Industrial societies, in contrast with developing nations, require innovation and commitment from many educated specialists in policy planning positions. And this type of commitment and innovation cannot be built on a foundation of terror and coercion.

Although in "closed" societies it is difficult to obtain data on competition and conflict, one of the persistent sources of friction *within* the Soviet Union and other socialist countries is the insistence of orthodox Party leaders on maintaining the methods of decision-making and conflict management that may have been appropriate for Lenin or Stalin, but that are certainly inappropriate in semistable industrialized societies. Much conflict *among* socialist countries results from the fact that the Soviet model of decision-making has been imposed (diffused) on other socialist countries without regard for their own peculiar situations. Czechoslovakia historically has been much more industrially developed and democratically inclined than the Soviet Union. The Soviet model of hierarchical control is clearly inappropriate from the Czech point of view, but it has been maintained through an invasion of Soviet troops in 1968 with disastrous results for the Czech economy. In Bulgaria, by contrast, the Soviet hierarchical model of control may be quite appropriate given the basic development problems that the Bulgarian leadership faces.

The pressures for citizen participation built into the industrialization process, with its social differentiation and pluralistic tendencies, are very important sources of conflict in socialist societies. The leadership of the CPSU and other communist parties has only hesitantly responded to these pressures for new *positions* of power, preferring instead to rely upon new economic *resources* (incentives) and coercion to maintain political control. Having made a decision not to decentralize authority and to deny broadened access to positions of power, however, older Party leaders are faced with an agenda of conflict management problems. One of them is suppression of dissent from those who are not easily silenced by withdrawal of economic rewards: among them a cultural and scientific elite that finds strict limits on dissent and attempts at thought control to be repulsive. Among these "catalysts for discontent" are Andrei Sakharov (father of the Russian H-Bomb), who has been periodically harassed for his outspoken views on intellectual freedom, and Alexander Solzhenitsyn, whose exaggerated novels critical of Stalinism were a thorn in the sides of Soviet leaders until he was asked to leave the country in 1974.[6]

While suppression of such dissent may be very painful to the individuals involved, it is much easier for political regimes to ostracize individuals than to suppress large-scale riots that could result from their activities.

There are many reasons that more orthodox communist party leaders attempt to retain hierarchical control and forego some of the conflict management advantages inherent in expanded political participation. There is obviously a significant element of fear involved. To open up previously closed political processes to widespread participation runs the risk of erosion of single party control, an uncomfortable prospect for present incumbents who are little experienced in the ways of open competition. Others, however, cling to these hierarchical models because they believe them to be ideologically correct. Finally, it is only human nature that those who have made it to the top within a set of understood rules of competition (or conflict) would not wish to see the system within which success has come significantly altered.

Managerial Politics

Because of regime readiness to use force to subdue dissent in most socialist countries, a distinction should be made between *actual* and *potential* political violence. There is little quantifiable political violence in these countries because it is foolhardy for individuals and groups to engage in the types of demonstrations that may be tolerated in more democratic countries. But this does not mean that the socialist citizen is necessarily happy with present incumbents or that there is not a great deal of discontent. In fact, there is much evidence to the contrary. The tensions and potential violence stemming from unmet demands for decentralization and meaningful citizen participation in determining collective policies lead to exaggerated regime dependence on a wide variety of conflict management tactics. These stress material incentives and propaganda and agitation to build citizen commitment that might otherwise result from meaningful participation.[7]

From the time of the Russian Revolution until the death of Stalin in 1953 there was little hesitance in the Soviet Union to insure stability through brute force used against unruly citizens. Workers unwilling to work twelve hours each day or farmers unwilling to join collective farms were liquidated or sent to prisons in Siberia as a reminder to others who might have similar ideas. Even within the Communist Party of the Soviet Union those who suggested a more open discussion of Marxist-Leninist principles found themselves in prison or facing firing squads. Incredible social costs, including death or imprisonment for millions of people, were paid in order that a very few within the CPSU could continue to allocate values for the many. A powerful secret police network pervaded Soviet society and frequent arrests kept even those who did no wrong in constant fear of a midnight knock on the door. While terror and coercion could insure compliance, they did little to increase regime legitimacy.[8]

Stalin exported his hierarchical model of political control to Eastern Europe on the heels of advancing Soviet troops at the end of World War II. He installed his favorite Eastern European communists, usually Moscow-trained party officials, in power in each Eastern European capital. During the late 1940s and early 1950s all of these societies were put through the Soviet-induced crucible of coercion. Beginning with the "Polish October" and the Hungarian revolution in 1956, however, Eastern European political leaders have slowly and irregularly moved away from coercion and toward consensus as a means of maintaining authority. At present there are great variations in the degree to which ruling political elites in these countries depend upon responsiveness to citizen demands and creation of consensus as managerial tactics. Yugoslav, Polish, and Hungarian leaders seem most responsive to citizen demands while East German, Soviet, Bulgarian, and Czechoslovakian leaders are least responsive.[9]

The Twentieth Congress of the Communist Party of the Soviet Union, held in 1956, marked a turning point in Soviet techniques of conflict management. Nikita Khrushchev delivered his famous "secret speech" in which he denounced Stalin and Stalinist methods of control. Following the speech many of Stalin's victims, particularly those already in the grave, were "rehabilitated" as part of a general condemnation of terror as a method of governing. Rehabilitation of dead victims was, from a cynical perspective, an inexpensive way of building support for the Khrushchev regime. Since the Twentieth Party Congress a serious effort has been made to develop some type of collegial rule within the Communist Party of the Soviet Union and within other ruling communist parties. There has also been a marked relaxation of the social tension that accompanied Stalinist excesses, a major effort to build regime legitimacy, increased public support for the CPSU, and a renewed effort to build utilitarian and moral citizen commitment to goals of the political regime.[10]

A commitment to the reduction of terror in managing conflict has meant redoubling of other conflict management techniques. All socialist regimes, for example, now rely heavily upon economic incentives to build citizen commitment. These incentives range from piecework systems of compensation (wages paid according to amount produced) designed to increase factory production to greater emphasis on press reports of socialist economic "progress" as a more general method of building public support. Various types of symbolic rewards, such as "hero of socialist labor" are used to create a new moral reward structure and identification with leadership goals based upon socialist principles. Attempts to create a new socialist consensus through control of educational curricula, mass media, and a network of youth groups play an important role. Although outright terror is now rarely used, there are a wide variety of more subtle control mechanisms that serve as substitutes. These include harassment of selected dissidents, including exile if necessary, and carefully calculated displays of force in dealing with dissident groups. In 1974, for example, Soviet leaders sent bulldozers through an "avante garde" art display in Moscow. No one was seriously injured, but the incident got the Party's message across.

Party leaders in the Soviet Union and Eastern Europe attempt to build regime support and manage conflict through various forms of what could be called *sham political competition*. Political leaders now go through the motions of encouraging broadened political participation without actually changing essential rules of government. For example, all citizens in the Soviet Union are required by law to vote on election day. Only those who are seriously ill can safely stay home and they are likely to be visited by volunteers who bring ballots to them. A tremendous amount of propaganda surrounds elections. Posters are put up, banners are hung, speeches are made, and eventually representatives are elected to the soviets (legislatures) on several levels. But most of the candidates for the Supreme Soviet (the highest legislative body) have been picked previously by CPSU nominating committees. A large portion of the public does get meaningfully involved in politics through candidacy for *local* offices, however. In 1965 over two million individuals were elected to positions in local government.¹¹ Local elections draw large numbers of people into politics and give them a feeling of political efficacy (effectiveness) at the local level even though they may not play a significant role in the national ruling political elite.

Soviet national elections are relatively insignificant as competitive events. Voters at the polls are presented with a list of nominees equal to the number of offices available. The only way that voters can express disfavor with any of these candidates is by crossing the candidate's name from the list. Nominees not receiving fifty percent of the vote are not elected. In general, nominees receive more than ninety-nine percent of the votes cast.[12] The nomination process is obviously the crucial competitive event, as receiving a nomination is tantamount to being elected. Nominations are made by trade unions, collective farms, the CPSU, and by other public organizations. A district electoral commission approves or rejects candidates. It is here that the CPSU exerts its control over the electoral process by staffing electoral commissions with loyal Party members.

A variation on the Soviet method is used in Poland and some open competition has been thus introduced into Polish politics. There are three recognized political parties in Poland and ballots contain a greater number of names than the number of positions to be filled. Candidates receiving the least number of votes fail to get elected. This electoral competition gives the voter some feeling that elections are meaningful because there is an opportunity to reject the least desirable of the candidates. But the slate of candidates is controlled by the Polish United Workers Party and lists are fixed so that it always wins a majority in the Polish Sejm (legislature).

Another technique that is used to create opportunities for upwardly mobile politicians is *frequent turnover of office holders*. This is a nonviolent substitute for the so-called permanent purge that was used by Stalin to keep his subordinates off balance and to open up new opportunities for loyal followers within the Party.[13] During the Stalinist era those removed from office were usually executed. More recently, however, rotation of top CPSU leadership was officially prescribed in the Party rules. The rules decreed that no less than one-quarter of the membership of the Central Committee and the Politbureau should be turned over at each election and that a larger portion of office holders should be rotated at lower levels. In practice this was much violated, particularly high in the Party hierarchy, and more recently these rotation requirements have been dropped, although rotation in office is still officially encouraged. The rotation rules represented a clever blend of apparent democratization under Party control. Since the rules were never enforced at the highest levels, top Party leaders remained immune. At lower levels, the Party used rotation to weed out the disloyal and incompetent. There can be no doubt, however, that turnover rules also injected democratization into the Party, particularly on the local level.

A bloodless relative of the permanent purge has been used recently in Eastern Europe, particularly in Poland and Czechoslovakia. Since the number of important positions available for allocation within the Party and state apparatus is limited by regime refusal to decentralize decision-making, competition can be insured and dissatisfaction minimized by periodically choosing scapegoats to be singled out for criticism and dismissal. This opens up positions for upwardly mobile and loyal party members, prevents conspiracies from developing, and keeps those who retain their jobs from becoming too self-confident. In Czechoslovakia first "Stalinist" and then "liberal" enemies of the people were removed from high office during the late 1960s. In Poland the outbreak of the first Arab-Israeli war in 1967 offered the leadership of the Polish United Workers Party an opportunity to remove high ranking officials from power, mostly Jews who had some ties to the Soviet Union, ostensibly because of their sympathies for Israel. This move permitted former party leader Wladyslaw Gomulka to rid himself of liberal critics, demote pro-Soviet officials, assign blame for economic failures, and to open up new positions for upwardly mobile, loyal young technocrats.[14]

Building Future Consensus

Socialist political leaders complement these schemes for maintaining their hierarchical models of decision-making with significant *political indoctrination* in schools and government-sponsored youth groups. These political socialization efforts are designed to enhance regime legitimacy by building moral commitment to socialism and to ruling socialist oligarchies within future generations. Political indoctrination takes place in all political systems including, of course, Great Britain and the United States.[15] But because of the peculiar historical circumstances and developmental problems mentioned above, political indoctrination has been much more overt in the Soviet Union and Eastern Europe than it has been in the United States or Great Britain.

In politically and industrially developed democracies a long period of relatively satisfactory interactions between citizens and ruling political elites has usually resulted in an effective system of covert political socialization through which values congruent with the goals of ruling political elites are passed from one generation to the next. In the United States children have traditionally learned that the domestic version of mass democracy practiced is ideal, that capitalism is an excellent type of economic system, that industrial growth is progress, that revolutions are destructive and bad ideas, and, until recently, that the president of the United States and other political figures are good men. All of this normally takes place with very little political interference in socialization processes. In many other countries, however, because of unfavorable interactions between masses and present ruling political elites, because not enough time has been available to build political community, or because political leaders have been perceived as agents of foreign powers, political socialization has become more overt indoctrination. This is the case in the Soviet Union and Eastern Europe where significant human and material resources are spent annually to insure that the next generation of young citizens will be supportive of socialist regimes.

Soviet attempts to build support for the present political regime in the school system are made through prescribed curricula for children and special ideological training for teachers. Heavy emphasis is placed on political indoctrination for adults through continuing education.[16] Soviet authorities also make special efforts to create special childhood peer groups that are conducive to the development of socialist values. A network of youth groups has been organized to supplement or replace more natural peer groups. The Soviet child can begin his or her "political" career in the Octobrists, an organization designed for children from seven to nine years of age. The next step is membership in the Pioneers, which includes children from ten to fourteen years of age. The most important youth group, both in terms of building regime legitimacy through indoctrination and as a stepping stone to membership in the Communist Party, is the Komsomol, which includes in its membership "youths" ranging in age from fourteen to twenty-eight years.

Studies of the success of consensus building and enhancement of regime legitimacy in socialist societies through political indoctrination have revealed that such programs yield mixed results. In a study of the Soviet youth program Kassof has reported that success is modest, at best. He claims that this is due to a basic contradiction in purpose. Youths are encouraged to join youth organizations because of the broad range of educational and recreational opportunities that membership offers. These groups receive much greater member support and loyalty when their members are permitted a key role in organization management. But the CPSU is not about to give control of activities to members. Ideological efforts thus often overshadow the educational and recreational role of Octobrist, Pioneer, and Komsomol units. Widespread disenchantment, erosion of rules, falsification of meeting minutes, and apathy have resulted from tight Party control.[17]

The experience in other socialist countries is very similar. In Poland, for example, in a sizable sample of university students who were members of youth groups, almost all claimed to belong to them only for instrumental reasons.[18] The indoctrination of young persons in these countries is in many ways less efficient than in the Soviet Union.

While there is much evidence that the effectiveness of *political* indoctrination has been limited, efforts to create a new *social consensus* seem to be more successful. Bronfenbrenner has found that Soviet youths have developed a much deeper social conscience and more concern for the welfare of the collective than their American counterparts. The price that has been paid, however, seems to be lack of individual initiative and an extraordinarily high level of individual conformity to group norms.[19] Other empirical studies carried out in Eastern Europe indicate that children in socialist countries are quite accepting of new social values associated with Marxism while they do not necessarily identify these values with political incumbents.[20] Data collected in Poland in the 1960s, when Wladyslaw Gomulka was still in power, indicate that children from worker and peasant families are most likely to accept egalitarian values. Children from these more educationally deprived backgrounds are also more likely to consider themselves Marxists than are those from more educated families. In addition, students choosing polytechnic training and looking forward to careers in business and industry are much *less* Marxist and egalitarian than are their counterparts following humanistic courses of study in the universities.[21]

CREATING A NEW REALITY

Control of the mass media is another aspect of conflict management that is particularly visible in socialist political systems. No regime permits the media to gather and disseminate information with complete impunity. Freedom of the press is supposedly cherished in Great Britain and the United States, as it supposedly is in the Soviet Union, but subtle and not so subtle political pressures define the limits of information that can be openly disseminated via the media. In the United States the Nixon administration's persistent attempts to modify facts and to inject its own version of "truth" into the media led to a serious "credibility gap" in the early 1970s. In spite of constitutional guarantees of media freedom in the Soviet Union and other socialist countries, censorship of radio, television, newspaper, and magazine content is understood to be part of the political game. But communist party leaders have found it difficult to change values and attitudes effectively and to construct a new reality through news manipulation.

Glavlit (Main Administration for Literary Affairs and Publishing) is officially in charge of censorship in the Soviet Union. It has counterparts in other socialist countries. Glavlit may prohibit the publication and distribution of works containing propaganda against Soviet authorities and the Dictatorship of the Proletariat, works that contain state secrets, works that arouse nationalistic or religious "fanaticism," or works that are defined as pornographic.[22] All printed materials, with the exception of Party papers, documents, etc., are technically subject to censorship before reaching the newsstand.

Throughout Soviet history blank columns on the front pages of daily newspapers and other types of obvious tampering gave testimony to Glavlit censorship. At present, Glavlit concerns itself more with military than political matters. Political censorship is now more subtle and most of it takes place informally. There is a loose set of "understood" standards specifying the types of materials that may be printed or broadcast. Whereas an editor or newscaster might be able to circumvent these standards occasionally, to do so on a regular basis would bring government and party pressures for dismissal. Thus, censorship is presently enforced more out of fear of loss of employment, reputation, etc. than by any precensorship or fear of a firing squad.[23]

There are a number of social and psychological factors that limit the ability to create consensus via information control. Although the Soviet, Polish, or Czech citizen is constantly exposed to ideologically approved information through the mass media, this does not mean that the message has a great impact. There are very real limits on the use of censorship as a conflict management tool. No socialist information system can ever be completely closed. Most socialist countries, for example, are located within radio, or even television, range of western countries. Socialist public opinion studies show that where external sources of information are available a substantial percentage of the listening audience uses them to check up on "official" versions of the news.[24] But the socialist citizen does not indiscriminately accept information from Radio Free Europe, the Voice of America, or the British Broadcasting Company. This information is treated with as much skepticism as that which originates internally, and objective "truth" is taken to lie somewhere between the official and foreign versions of the news.

Another information management limitation is imposed by tourism. Each year hundreds of thousands of tourists move freely to and from socialist countries and there are ample opportunities for citizens to check the veracity of state-provided news. The only way to control this flow of information would be to stem tourism, an unlikely prospect because of the hard currency produced by the tourist industry.

Another factor limiting the effectiveness of information management is the "two-step" nature of communication networks. Most individuals do not turn directly to the mass media for information. Rather, information is filtered through other people who act as media "gatekeepers." Survey research studies have shown other people to be extremely important sources of information in communist countries. Interviews with Russian refugees in the early 1950s revealed that more than one-third of the respondents had relied on "word of mouth" as their most trusted source of information when they were in the Soviet Union.[25] More recent surveys in Poland have shown that more than forty percent of those interviewed reported "other people" to be an important source of information about foreign and domestic events.[26]

Rumor finds fertile soil in which to spread in semiclosed communications systems. In both the Soviet Union and Eastern Europe officials periodically are hard pressed to deny rumors generated by unofficial "sources" in which citizens place great trust. When citizens feel that news is distorted by political pressures they are much more willing to lend credence to a wide variety of rumors than they are to official pronouncements.

Education is also important in limiting the effectiveness of information management. More intense media management efforts are required to indoctrinate more educated and sophisticated audiences. In Poland, for example, recent survey research has revealed that forty percent of those with a higher education frequently find themselves critical of the press, thirty-one percent with secondary school educations find themselves critical, while only twenty-two percent possessing an elementary school education or less are frequently critical of the press.[27] While political regimes engaging in information distortion may be able to successfully create false information for some of the people some of the time, it is more difficult to manipulate information when it is destined for an educated and sophisticated audience.

Although their effectiveness in outright propaganda and censorship is limited, it should also be emphasized that journals and newspapers in socialist countries manage conflict in other ways. They represent the positions of political interest groups and act as political safety valves. Many papers are recognized as organs for professional groups and editorial policies reflect group opinion. In the Soviet Union *Trud* represents the views of labor, *Krasnaya Zvezda* the military, *Pravda* the party central committee, *Literaturnaya Gazeta* the intellectuals, etc. While no sensible newspaper or journal editor would publish an editorial attacking high-ranking Party officials, there are many ways of carrying out political infighting more subtly. Condemnations of "rightest" or "leftist" tendencies within communist parties represent veiled attacks against certain political leaders. More direct editorial attacks against low-level bureaucrats for incompetence are often made in the press. And these editorials are not without influence or impact.

The socialist press also undertakes its own investigations based upon letters of complaint from readers. Producers of shoddy merchandise, purveyors of spoiled produce, or nonresponsive officials are likely to find themselves targets of press investigations which often result in political roastings. These investigations help reduce citizen frustration because it appears to those making complaints that someone is taking them seriously.

The letters-to-the-editor policies of many major socialist newspapers is a related tension reduction device. Readers are encouraged to send letters of complaint and sizable editorial staffs deal with them. In the Soviet Union *Pravda* receives over 300,000 letters annually and *Izvestia* has received as many as half a million. Careful selection of representative letters can be very effective in dampening potential conflict even though nothing may actually result from their publication. More often, however, letters to the editor do result in some sort of policy change. Careful management of letters-to-the-editor selection can also play an important role in ongoing political struggles. In many respects the pen is now mightier than the sword in socialist political competition, and many political dramas are played out on the editorial pages of journals and newspapers.

COMPETITION IN THE NEW CLASS

Because there are no fully competitive electoral campaigns among political parties in socialist countries as there are in the United States or Great Britain and because the Supreme Soviet and other socialist legislatures are really powerless as legislative bodies, political competition among groups in the Soviet Union and other socialist societies is not readily apparent or easily observed. In fact, we do not really know the dimensions of group-based political competition or the relative power of any particular group in socialist politics. Open conflict is usually quickly suppressed in these countries and information about it is also very incomplete. For a considerable period after Stalin's death specialists in Soviet studies wrote as if the Soviet political system was monolithic and under the control of one or two individuals. Indeed, there is still no clear consensus on the role that group competition or conflict plays in Soviet politics, although it is generally conceded that the "totalitarian" model of Soviet politics suggested by Friederick and Brzezinski is not a valid picture of Soviet politics.[28]

Studies of interest group activity in Soviet politics have been pioneered by Skilling.[29] According to Skilling, the Soviet political system has been undergoing a deep transition since Stalin's death. A very important part of this transition has been increased political competition among various interest groups. There has also been broadened group participation in many of the stages of

Conflict Management Under Socialism

policy-making. While the CPSU still retains tight control over major decisions within its Politbureau and Central Committee, specialized groups such as enterprise managers, engineers, economists, military officers, etc. have developed their own political interests. In fact, many important persons in these groups occupy positions both within them and also as high ranking Party members. The same is true in other socialist countries. Strategically placed elites within socialist societies also make decisions through noncompliance or minimal compliance with Party directives. This "quiet veto" is very important in complex societies where it is impossible for a small group at the top to monitor compliance with directives effectively.

Groups possessing real or potential power in Soviet political competition have been the subject of investigations by a number of scholars. Economists are foremost among the groups studied. Party leaders place heavy emphasis on rapid economic growth as a way of creating resources to enhance regime legitimacy since satisfied consumers make poor revolutionaries (or counterrevolutionaries). This economic imperative is well understood by political incumbents and it means that economists have a privileged role in economic decision-making. While it would be difficult for an economist to argue for decentralization of power based on ideological principles, it is much more acceptable to the Party if an argument is made on grounds of economic rationality or economic efficiency. This has been the case in protracted debates over the "Liberman Plan" for reducing centralized economic planning.

Economists' ideas are expounded in journals and newspapers, at professional gatherings, and at public meetings and debates. The academies of science and major universities in socialist countries are particularly important sources of influence. Within these institutions, mathematical economists are very influential in policy decisions because of their ability to model complex economic systems in a logical manner, a procedure that is intellectually impressive to older Party members who often do not understand the essence of computer modeling.[30]

Enterprise managers and industrial bureaucrats are another privileged component of what Djilas has called the "new class."[31] They also are crucial to successful economic performance within socialist countries. By virtue of their backgrounds, education, training, etc. they tend to be a task-oriented homogeneous group.

In this respect they are not unlike Party members, but younger businessman-managers especially have interests of their own. They are primarily concerned with production efficiency and, in many cases, this aligns them with young economists in opposing a centralized command economy and the power of older political elites.

The new generation of managers competes or conflicts with older Party members on several important issues. Foremost among these is a perpetual political argument over allocation of resources between heavy and light industry. Many older Party members still live under mental Stalinism and stress the needs of defense and heavy industry. Younger managers are more interested in meeting consumer expectations through the rapid development of light industries. They also want greater autonomy, particularly in outlining long-term plans, setting quotas, purchasing raw materials, and in recruiting personnel. There are a number of other points of contention including the structure of rewards for factory managers (the size of salaries and bonuses) and the development of management as a profession apart from Party control.[32]

The ultimate political power of industrial managers is negative in nature. They can sabotage Party directives and Party leaders are limited in their ability to retaliate because of the need to keep industrial management economically productive. As a result the managerial class has its own domain within which it can exercise considerable influence. But this influence diminishes outside the domain of factory planning.[33]

The evolution of socialist politics in Yugoslavia has been much different from that in the Soviet Union. Although politics is still dominated by one party, the League of Communists, an effort has been made to institutionalize various types of inter-elite conflicts within existing political structures. The Yugoslav constitution also recognizes the importance, and even legitimacy, of regional cleavages and gives a great deal of autonomy to the six constituent republics. The Federal Assembly is bicameral with a Federal Council elected to represent interests of all citizens and a Council of Producers elected to represent interests of various occupational groups. It is understood that regions and groups may legitimately have divergent interests, and a substantial amount of potential violence is reduced to competition within these legislative structures.

Conflict Management Under Socialism

An effort has also been made in Yugoslavia to create conditions under which the state could "wither away." Political and economic institutions have been decentralized to a much greater extent than in other socialist countries. Control of industrial enterprises is in the hands of Worker's Councils which are responsible for determining enterprise policies. Yugoslav communes, local units of administration, have considerable autonomy, and citizen participation in commune decision-making is heavy.

The Yugoslav road to socialism seems to have fostered citizen commitment to socialist values. Zaninovich has found no significant gap between elite and mass verbal commitment to socialist ideology in Yugoslavia.[34] Furthermore, he found little difference in values between specialist and professional elites, which contrasts with data for the Soviet Union. It seems that the Yugoslav participatory pluralist path to socialism is one that inspires commitment and develops social consensus.

The military plays an important role in determining allocations in the Soviet Union just as it does in the United States. In both countries military expenditures represent a substantial portion of all public expenditures. In recent years the United States has been spending about six percent of its total gross national product on the military, an average of about $375 for each citizen. The Soviet Union spends a similar portion on military affairs, averaging about $275 per person.[35]

The political power and competitive position of the military is based on the fact that national defense is a primary concern in budgetary allocations. Thus, the generals are quite influential in political affairs. The leadership of the CPSU is well aware of the need to curry military favor as the military is the ultimate source of power in the case of internal threats to the present regime. Thus, since 1939 the military has consistently made up about ten percent of the Central Committee of the CPSU. While many interest groups in Soviet politics agitate for change, the military usually lines up with more conservative elements and opposes any significant shifts in allocations.[36]

There are other important interest groups in Soviet and Eastern European politics. The Party *apparatchiki* themselves represent a collection of interests.[37] The cultural intelligentsia, writers, actors, directors, journalists, etc., also play a significant role in influencing public opinion and political competition. They have regularly argued for more intellectual freedom and significant political reforms. Educators and social scientists represent groups that could play a much more significant role in the formation of future social policies.

It should be stressed that even though these interest groups seem to be important in socialist politics, competition takes place within the closed hierarchy of ruling communist parties. Also, much of what is known about group conflict and competition has been intuited from an inadequate information base. But in comparison with Stalinist times, it seems that Politbureaus and Central Committees are more open to discussion, debate, and influence from groups within and outside the ruling parties and that the nature of political competition and conflict in socialist societies is slowly changing. The potential for the development of pluralist competition presently exists, but the degree to which this potential pluralism turns into pluralist democracy remains to be seen.

THE END OF IDEOLOGY?

Ideological fervor has been a constant source of violence and recrimination in socialist politics as well as in relations between the socialist bloc and other countries. In the past ideology has been at least partially responsible for the deaths and imprisonment of millions. Indeed, ideological fervor is one of the reasons that communism has been so much feared in nonsocialist countries.

Social differentiation, specialization, and rationalization have been discussed in Chapter 3 as industrialization-related processes that produce pluralist tendencies in modernizing societies. Socialist industrialization is also subject to these processes. Their impact on authority relationships in socialist countries is imperfectly understood, but a logical hypothesis would be that such pluralist tendencies will lead to further decentralization of responsibility, broader-based recruitment of political elites, continued decline of ideologies, and perhaps more democratic methods of reaching collective decisions.

Welsh has suggested that the rapid growth of bureaucracy in socialist countries has led to a decline in the importance of ideological considerations in decision-making, increased use of rational-technical criteria in recruitment of elites, and the emergence of a new industrial-managerial class.[38] It is generally accepted that ideology has been on the wane since the death of

Conflict Management Under Socialism

Stalin. Ideology has lost its importance as a prescription for the authoritative allocation of values. Brzezinski claims that ideology now plays only a "rationalizing" role in socialist decision-making.[39] It justifies decisions that have been made and sets rules of socialist competition even though its tenets do not actually play a crucial role in policy formation.

This decline in the importance of ideology is one result of recruitment of increasing numbers of technical specialists into the ruling political elite. Efficiency needs of highly industrialized societies require ruling communist parties to co-opt such technical expertise into policy-making processes. Thus, the "technocracy" that results seems to be a requisite for optimal decision-making at advanced levels of industrialization, and communist party ideologues are forced to make compromises.[40]

A new managerial class is another result of industrialization and specialization needs in socialist societies. Djilas and Popovic have argued that this "new class" has developed interests of its own quite apart from communist parties and that this is also responsible for the decline in ideological orthodoxy.[41] While men in "gray flannel suits" are not necessarily democrats, a unified managerial class represents a privileged group with vested interests that is quite capable of checking the arbitrary exercise of power by nonspecialist party politicians.

While the argument that task differentiation and specialization inherent in industrialization will lead to the "convergence" (development of similarities) of political authority systems at advanced levels of industrialization does not seem yet to be sustained by adequate data, it is clear that the needs of industrial societies for managerial expertise militates against the maintenance of Stalinist hierarchical models of decision-making. Industrial societies require at least minimum consensus and citizen commitment if political stability and economic productivity are to be maintained.[42] While building consensus certainly requires some decentralization of responsibility and relaxation of coercion, steps that are apparently being taken in many socialist countries, this does not mean that western-style liberal democracy is just around the corner. It does mean, however, that the importance of ideology will undoubtedly decline further and that various forms of semiparticipatory, pluralist political systems will continue to evolve in Eastern Europe and the Soviet Union. This evolution will undoubtedly be accompanied by more open expression of the conflict and competition that previously has been suppressed.

REFERENCES

1. The merits, drawbacks, and necessities of Stalin's methods are discussed in A. Nove, *Was Stalin Really Necessary?: Some Problems of Soviet Political Economy*. London: Allen and Unwin, 1964.
2. Detail on the extent of the purges is found in D. Lane, *Politics and Society in the U.S.S.R.* New York: Random House, 1970, p. 77.
3. See A. Nove, "The Soviet Model and Underdeveloped Countries," in C. Welch, ed., *Political Modernization*. Belmont, Calif.: Wadsworth, 1967.
4. For a theoretical treatment of the effectiveness of various types of controls in different situations see A. Etzioni, *A Comparative Analysis of Complex Organizations*. New York: Free Press, 1961, ch. 4.
5. The basic motivation for slave labor is a desire to live. Slave labor can be effectively used where quantifiable task performance can be linked to survival. Thus, food and shelter can be parceled out in relation to task performance.
6. See A. Sakharov, *Progress, Coexistence, and Intellectual Freedom*. New York: Norton, 1968; A. Solzhenitsyn, *Cancer Ward*. New York: Bantam Books, 1969; A. Solzhenitsyn, *The First Circle*. New York: Bantam Books, 1969.
7. Etzioni, *A Comparative Analysis of Complex Organizations*, ch. 1.
8. More detail on the role of terror in historical socialist construction is found in R. Conquest, *The Great Terror: Stalin's Purge of the Thirties*. New York: Macmillan, 1968.
9. D. Pirages, "Socioeconomic Development and Political Access in the Communist Party States," in J. Triska, ed., *Communist Party States: Comparative and International Studies*. Indianapolis: Bobbs-Merrill, 1969.
10. See Etzioni, *A Comparative Analysis of Complex Organizations*, ch. 1, for more detailed analysis of utilitarian and moral compliance patterns.
11. Lane, *Politics and Society in the U.S.S.R.*, pp. 152ff.
12. For an analysis of Soviet election statistics and those who do not vote for approved candidates, see J. Gilison, "Soviet Elections as a Measure of Dissent: The Missing One Per Cent," *The American Political Science Review* (September 1968).
13. It should be stressed that rotation in office is certainly much more humane than the earlier permanent purges. Rotation in office can be viewed from two perspectives: as a device used by the Communist Party to manage those who obtain office or as a meaningful way of opening up political processes to greater citizen participation.

14. See P. Lendvai, *Anti-Semitism Without Jews*. Garden City, N.Y.: Doubleday, 1971, esp. pt. II.
15. For a comparison of methods of building legitimacy in Great Britain and the Soviet Union see J. Gilison, *British and Soviet Politics: Legitimacy and Convergence*. Baltimore: John Hopkins Press, 1972, esp. chs. 1 and 5.
16. See N. DeWitt, *Education and Professional Employment in the U.S.S.R.* Washington, D.C.: National Science Foundation, 1961; E. Mickiewicz, *Soviet Political Schools*. New Haven: Yale University Press, 1967.
17. A. Kassof, *The Soviet Youth Program*. Cambridge: Harvard University Press, 1965, chs. 6 and 8.
18. This is one general conclusion in an unpublished study of Warsaw University students carried out in the mid-1960s. S. Novak et al., *Studenci Warszawy*. Warsaw: University of Warsaw, unpublished manuscript.
19. U. Bronfenbrenner, *Two Worlds of Childhood*. New York: Russell Sage Foundation, 1970, ch. 3.
20. Novak et al., *Studenci Warszawy*.
21. D. Pirages, *Modernization and Political Tension Management: A Socialist Society in Perspective*. New York: Praeger, 1972, pp. 94ff.
22. M. Hopkins, *Mass Media in the Soviet Union*. New York: Pegasus, 1970, pp. 78–79.
23. See Hopkins, *Mass Media in the Soviet Union*, ch. 3, and G. Hollander, *Soviet Political Indoctrination: Developments in Mass Media and Propaganda since Stalin*. New York: Praeger, 1972.
24. A. Sicinski, *Funkje Informacyjne Prasy i Radia*. Warsaw: Osrodek Badania Opinii Publicznej, 1959.
25. A. Inkeles and R. Bauer, *The Soviet Citizen*. New York: Atheneum, 1968, pp. 161–65.
27. Sicinski, *Funkje Informacyjne Prasy i Radia*.
28. C. Friedrick and Z. Brzezinski, *Totalitarian Dictatorship and Autocracy*. New York: Praeger, 1966.
29. G. Skilling and F. Griffiths, eds., *Interest Groups in Soviet Politics*. Princeton: Princeton University Press, 1971, esp. chs. 1 and 10.
30. R. Judy, "The Economists," in Skilling and Griffiths, *Interest Groups in Soviet Politics*.
31. M. Djilas, *The New Class*. New York: Praeger, 1954.
32. J. Hardt and T. Frankel, "The Industrial Managers," in Skilling and Griffiths, *Interest Groups in Soviet Politics*.
33. See J. Azrael, *Managerial Power and Soviet Politics*. Cambridge: Harvard University Press, 1966.
34. G. Zaninovich, "Elites and Citizenry in Yugoslav Society: A Study of Value Differentiation," in C. Beck et al., *Comparative Communist Political Leadership*. New York: McKay, 1973.

35. *World Military Expenditures 1971*. Washington, D.C.: United States Arms Control and Disarmament Agency, 1972.
36. R. Kolkowicz, "The Military," in Skilling and Griffiths, *Interest Groups in Soviet Politics*.
37. M. Lodge, "Attitudinal Cleavages within the Soviet Political Leadership," in Beck et al., *Comparative Communist Political Leadership*. See also J. Hough, "The Party Apparatchiki," in Skilling and Griffiths, *Interest Groups in Soviet Politics*, and J. Hough, *The Soviet Prefects: The Local Party Organs in Industrial Decision-Making*. Cambridge: Harvard University Press, 1969.
38. W. Welsh, "The Comparative Study of Political Leadership in Communist Systems," in Beck et al., *Comparative Communist Political Leadership*.
39. Z. Brzezinski, "The Nature of the Soviet Union," in Z. Brzezinski, ed., *Ideology and Power in the Soviet Union*. New York: Praeger, 1967.
40. See Welsh, "The Comparative Study of Political Leadership in Communist Systems," pp. 3ff.
41. Djilas, *The New Class*. See also N. Popovic, *Yugoslavia: The New Class in Crisis*. Syracuse: Syracuse University Press, 1968, for a more critical follow-up to the Djilas book.
42. See Pirages, *Modernization and Political Tension Management*, chs. 6 and 7.

6
THE FUTURE AND POLITICAL CONFLICT

Theories of political conflict and competition have concentrated mainly on social and psychological variables in seeking to explain conflict behavior. Although these social and psychological factors are obviously very important, most studies have neglected the physical environment linkages that give rise to social phenomena. Prior to the twentieth century the number of human beings in relation to the physical environment's sustaining capacity was rather small. Now, however, population pressures, crowding, pollution, depletion of mineral resources, etc. all loom much larger in explanations of political competition and conflict.

Political conflict is conditioned by *both* physical and social environments. The physical environment, which consists of such things as mineral resources, agricultural land, rainfall, etc., places constraints on economic and, indirectly, political possibilities. Democratic political systems, for example, have been rare because democracy does not work well when resources are scarce and populations are pressing against environmental limitations. Social environments, including economic factors, also constrain political possibilities. Fundamental disagreement over basic values, conflicts among ethnic or religious groups, or lack of industrial development can severely restrict development of regime legitimacy or democracy. Social and physical environments, however, are closely related. Physical environmental conditions establish parameters within which social developments take place. And socioeconomic conditions are very important in determining attitudes toward the physical environment.

Political science has developed as a discipline in an atmosphere of economic expansion in societies of relative abundance. The dominant assumptions guiding social and political research have stressed the goodness, inevitability, and persistence of economic growth as a factor smoothing over conflict and encouraging the development of democratic competition.

In the 1970s increasing awareness of physical environmental constraints rooted in a series of resource and environmental problems has slowly begun to change the abundance perspective. Levels of population, technology, and access to natural resources are now recognized as important variables in determining conflict among nations.[1] The inevitability or desirability of increased consumption of resources is no longer universally accepted, and a politics of a "steady-state," a condition in which consumption of natural resources would be sharply reduced in keeping with environmental imperatives, has been outlined.[2] The political research of abundance is slowly changing and a number of new perspectives on political man and the future of political conflict and conflict management under conditions of slowed growth are being examined.

POST-INDUSTRIAL SOCIETY—CONFLICT AND CONSENSUS

Post-industrial is a term that has been used to describe a transition to an advanced stage of industrial development based upon increasing use of computers, new communications technologies, and miniaturization. This contrasts with the initial round of industrialization with its heavy emphasis on automation and fossil-fuel-based production of goods.[3] Most projections of a post-industrial political future have indicated a diminution of conflict. Science and technology have been seen as benevolent forces that will continue to reshape the physical environment in response to new economic demands. A few, more pessimistic, scenarios have also been sketched out, but they have understandably not caught public attention, being looked upon as science fiction rather than as a realistic vision of the future.[4]

One of the most detailed and typically optimistic projections of political and socioeconomic conditions in a post-industrial society has been made by Daniel Bell.[5] He has identified the following five dimensions of change in moving from industrial to post-industrial societies.

1. A transition to post-industrial society is marked by a *shift from production of goods to production of services*.[6] In early stages of industrialization blue collar job opportunities open up in manufacturing. The post-industrial economy, by contrast, is characterized by rapid growth of white collar employment in services, both personal services such as banking, health, retail sales, and personal

hygiene and public services such as government, education, and research. Implicit in Bell's work is a belief that conflict over the allocation of resources and positions will decrease as the service sector expands. Post-industrial society will be marked by abundance and a revolution of rising expectations will be satiated by new productivity.

2. Bell's post-industrial society is also characterized by a *marked change in occupational and social structure*.[7] In post-industrial society an urban proletariat is replaced by a rising technical and managerial class, a "technocracy," that is much more highly educated in comparison with the urban proletariat. This technocracy derives considerable satisfaction from its work and becomes "preeminent" in the post-industrial setting. Post-industrial class politics becomes a politics of technocrats and managers. Ideological and value clashes give way to discussions of method as the values of the technocrats become those of society.

3. *The primacy of theoretical knowledge and its application to a wide variety of problems* is a third attribute of post-industrial society.[8] Post-industrial development is organized around knowledge. Advanced methods of communication, consumer research, computer analysis, and information retrieval become essential components of a new society in which an information revolution is responsible for more rational approaches to solving social problems.

4. *Planning and control of technological growth* represents the fourth of Bell's significant differences between industrial and post-industrial society.[9] The unplanned and undirected growth characteristic of early stages of laissez-faire economic development gives way to long-term planning. The power of planners within bureaucracies is enhanced as pressures increase for development and use of technology assessment on a regular basis to replace the "indeterminancy" associated with past technological developments.

5. The final aspect of post-industrial society is the *rise of a new intellectual technology*.[10] Bell here refers to a new kit of tools or methods with which problem-solving can be approached. The problems of post-industrial society are those of organized complexity brought on by the management of very large and complex systems. Intuitive judgment is replaced by sets of rules for solving problems. Obviously, the power of a new techno-managerial class, aided by computers and new rules of inquiry, is enhanced and the role of politicians as brokers and representatives of conflicting

interests diminishes in the face of "rational policies rationally arrived at."

Accepting this utopian view of post-industrial harmony would seemingly lead to the conclusion that the sources of political conflict would disappear. In a rational society of abundance run by experts the end of ideology would be at hand. Continually growing economic productivity would obviate traditional economic struggles over distribution of resources. The technocracy responsible for production and distribution of knowledge would play a much greater role in rational decision-making processes and would replace the selfish competition inherent in interest group liberalism. *Rational* political decisions would thus be made by *rational* and educated leadership in an atmosphere of abundance and a more *rational* citizenry would accept those decisions.

Such rosy visions of the future society and political system have ignored changes in the physical environment that may prove just as, or even more, important than the trends that have been seized upon by optimistic futurists. They assume that continuing material prosperity will reduce political conflict. But this is far from obvious for two reasons. New types of sociopolitical expectations may shift struggles over tangible resources to conflict over less tangible values and prestige positions. In addition, there are very real questions about the ability of the physical environment, including the earth's resource base, to sustain the projected industrial growth leading to post-industrial affluence. Both changing social expectations and physical environmental limits to growth could serve to continue, or even intensify, the political conflict and competition that presently pervades industrial societies.

Rediscovering the Physical Environment

The physical environment and its impact on social life have been much ignored by the social sciences. Aside from emphasis on geography as a causal variable in international conflict, the link between environmental abundance or scarcity and political conflict has been overlooked. In historical perspective the 1970s may well be noted as the decade in which political scientists, as well as the rest of humanity, first took note of physical limits on economic growth as well as the close relationship that exists among resource abundance, industrial growth, and political stability. Industrialization has relied upon substitution of machines and energy released from nature's fossil fuel reserves to do the work that has formerly been done by human beings and beasts of burden. Machines, like human beings, need to be fed and their diet consists of energy produced by coal, petroleum, and natural gas. Industrial societies are now sustained by this "fossil fuel subsidy" of energy produced from hydrocarbons. As industrialization has reached out to embrace the whole planet and as the number of human beings has increased, demand for fossil fuels relative to known reserves has risen very rapidly, and once seemingly infinite reserves appear very finite indeed.[11]

The industrial revolution has created material prosperity previously unknown. Furthermore, this affluence has been created with an apparently decreasing amount of physical labor. During the industrial revolution it has appeared that people have been able to get *more* of a return for less expenditure of human effort. Political leaders in industrial countries have been able to promise two chickens in every pot or two Cadillacs in every garage, and increased worker productivity has permitted them to deliver. A politics of compromise has flourished in this atmosphere as one person's gain has not been another's loss.

Many dimensions of environmental limits to growth were concisely summarized in a 1972 study entitled *The Limits to Growth*. The study used computer models to project a series of likely planetary resource and environmental futures. The authors concluded that exponential growth in world population and consumption would soon place intolerable strains on natural disposal systems and the resource base that now sustain industrial civilization.[12]

Food is the most critical of these limits.[13] Food is necessary to meet the most basic of human needs and food shortages can rapidly lead to bloody confrontations. Population growth has forced many countries to bring "marginal" agricultural land into production. Opening this new land is both economically expensive and politically risky. It is expensive because of the costs of clearing, fertilizing, and irrigating marginal land. It is politically risky because marginal land is usually most vulnerable to shifts in weather patterns. Former Soviet Premier Nikita Khrushchev discovered the risks involved when he opened up marginal agricultural lands in the eastern part of the Soviet Union. After two or three years of good harvests, drought set in, upsetting normal patterns of food distribution. One of the issues upon which Khrushchev's enemies seized in order to oust him from power was his alleged "mishandling" of agricultural policy.

The world food problem is much more pressing in other countries. Famines in north central Africa and in India have recently created serious political instability. Conflict over food and land distribution forced dictator Haile Selassie of Ethiopia to step down in 1974 after decades of iron-fisted rule. Food riots are an accepted form of political conflict, or perhaps competition, in India, where food is perennially in short supply. In fact, food-related problems were among those leading to the establishment of "one-woman" rule in India in 1975. Furthermore, new technologies associated with the "green revolution," a method of increasing crop yields through genetic research on planets and intensive uses of fertilizer and pesticides, continue to exacerbate conflict over land distribution in many less-developed countries.

Fresh water represents a related limit to growth that has already become a source of conflict within and among nations. Despite an abundance of salt water in the oceans, only a limited supply of fresh water exists, originating as rainfall over the world's land masses. Human beings and their agriculture and industry require large amounts of water, and there are indications that needed amounts may not be available by the year 2000. In Europe, pollution of the Rhine River has made water dangerous for drinking in "downstream" countries, an enduring source of international discussion. Use of water in the Colorado River is a continuing source of friction between the United States and Mexico, which gets mineral-laden water that is "left over" after the United States irrigates upstream. A very high price must be paid for future water and considerable political conflict will surround disposition of the water that is available.

Global mineral resources represent another limit to growth and a potential source of international conflict. Fossil fuels and non-fuel minerals that were once relatively plentiful and cheap are becoming more expensive to discover and extract. Depletion-related politics can be expected to make the prices of basic commodities an issue between the industrial and less-developed world. Resource depletion is not necessarily the most critical factor shaping such conflict in the near future. The global distribution of resources is much more important. Countries richly endowed with minerals, particularly petroleum, will profit economically and politically from rising prices while countries less well endowed will suffer. It is significant in this respect that the Soviet Union is much more self-sufficient in mineral resources than is the United States.[14] Furthermore, most of Western Europe is now dependent upon the rest of the world for almost all essential minerals. A concerted holding action by resource "haves" against these resource "have-nots" would be a new and more subtle form of international conflict.

The continuing international energy crisis is a prime example of the political aspects of global resource depletion and distribution. Thirteen countries making up the Organization of Petroleum Exporting Countries (OPEC) now control about ninety percent of the world's petroleum exports. Since this cartel began using oil as an economic weapon, the political effects on the industrial world have been catastrophic. Not only has serious inflation been sparked by price increases for petroleum, but the possibility of industrial collapse and related political instability in some industrial democracies, such as Italy, seems very real.

In summary, the physical environment can be expected to influence political conflict and conflict management in the future in a number of ways. World food and mineral resource limitations in the face of increasing demand could spark economic inflation around the world. Inflation, in turn, could have serious social and political implications in many countries, and political battles could be fought over apportioning inflation's effects. Cycles of economic boom and bust may become more common as industrial countries find it impossible to maintain the high rates of industrial growth that have been characteristic of the recent past without succumbing to double-digit inflation. This may well exacerbate traditional social cleavages; labor against management, the old against the young, vested interests against the upwardly mobile, etc., as all struggle to keep wages, dividends, and welfare payments in line with spiraling costs of living. As economist Henry Wallich has concisely put it, "So long as there is growth, there is hope, and that makes large income differences tolerable."[15] In the absence of continued economic growth, political conflict over the distribution of a relatively constant stock of resources can be expected to intensify.

Managing Post-Industrial Complexity

Environmental pressures will be accompanied by changes in social organization that will also have an important impact on authority relationships in post-industrial societies. There seems to be general agreement that post-industrial society must be more interdependent and complex if high standards of living are to be maintained. It is questionable whether mass democracy as a way of making collective decisions can survive in the face of increasing environmental pressures and rising social expectations. It is also questionable whether social, political, and economic conflict such as strikes, boycotts, demonstrations, etc. can be tolerated within the new complexity.

In addition to these more obvious problems associated with growing interdependence and complexity, social and political malcontents can now throw "monkey wrenches" into the delicate social machinery that sustains high productivity. But new violence might not result from only *committed* acts, such as political kidnappings, sniper slayings, or construction of small nuclear devices with stolen plutonium, but also from *omitted* acts in which failures of individuals or groups to perform adequately inadvertently leads to the deaths of many other people. New technological developments, such as nuclear power plants, will only increase susceptibility to the "monkey wrench syndrome."

As long as the number of these "technological pressure points" remains small relative to a political system's capacity to regulate, adequate supervision may be possible. But it is certain that coordinating the complexity of post-industrial society, highly dependent upon nuclear power and other potentially lethal technologies, will require either a very high level of social consensus and political legitimacy or more coercive control. In a complex future society the perceived costs of deviance could escalate and tolerance for disruption could diminish. Although there is no way to predict future events precisely, particularly since human beings are capable of rationally altering them, the cornucopian view of a future of abundance and diminishing conflict must be tempered with a more realistic assessment of problems that could be created by *changing physical environmental conditions* and by the new *complexity of the social environment*.

REFERENCES

1. H. Sprout and M. Sprout, *Toward a Politics of the Planet Earth.* New York: Van Nostrand Reinhold Co., 1971; N. Choucri, *Population Dynamics and International Violence: Propositions, Insights, and Evidence.*, Lexington, Mass.: Heath, 1974; N. Choucri and

R. North, *Nations in Conflict: National Growth and International Violence*. San Francisco: W. H. Freeman, 1975.
2. W. Ophuls, "Leviathan or Oblivion," in Herman Daly, ed., *Toward A Steady-State Economy*. San Francisco: W. H. Freeman, 1973; D. Pirages and P. Ehrlich, *Ark II: Social Response to Environmental Imperatives*. San Francisco: W. H. Freeman, 1974.
3. See Z. Brzezinski, *Between Two Ages: America's Role in the Technetronic Era*. New York: Viking, 1970, pt. I.
4. See G. Stent, *The Coming of the Golden Age: A View of the End of Progress*. Garden City, N.Y.: Natural History Press, 1969; and R. Vacca, *The Coming Dark Age*. Garden City, N.Y.: Anchor Books, 1974.
5. D. Bell, *The Coming of Post-Industrial Society: A Venture in Social Forecasting*. New York: Basic Books, 1973.
6. Bell, *The Coming of Post-Industrial Society*, pp. 14–15.
7. Bell, *The Coming of Post-Industrial Society*, pp. 15–18.
8. Bell, *The Coming of Post-Industrial Society*, pp. 18–26.
9. Bell, *The Coming of Post-Industrial Society*, pp. 26–27.
10. Bell, *The Coming of Post-Industrial Society*, pp. 27–33.
11. See P. Ehrlich, A. Ehrlich, and J. Holdren, *Human Ecology: Problems and Solutions*. San Francisco: W. H. Freeman, 1973, and R. Falk, *This Endangered Planet*. New York: Random House, 1971.
12. D. Meadows et al. *The Limits to Growth*. New York: Universe Books, 1972. See also M. Mesarovich and E. Pestel, *Mankind at the Turning Point*. New York: Dutton, 1974.
13. G. Borgstrom, *The Hungry Planet: The Modern World at the Edge of Famine*. New York: Macmillan, 1965; and G. Borgstrom, *Focal Points: A Global Food Strategy*. New York: Macmillan, 1973.
14. D. Pirages, "Strategic Implications of the Energy Crisis." (Paper presented to the Annual Meeting of the International Studies Association, Washington, D.C., February 1975.)
15. H. Wallich, *Newsweek*, January 24 1972, p. 60.

7
CROSS-NATIONAL STUDIES OF CONFLICT: CONCEPTS AND METHODS

In the preceding chapters a diverse body of literature analyzing political conflict and conflict management in a number of different settings has been examined. The universe of related studies, ranging from those dealing with conflict among individuals to those involving conflict among nation-states, is obviously of unmanageable proportions, and only a sample of relevant studies could be considered. However, a "mainstream" of cross-national studies of conflict and violence has drawn very heavily on these disparate efforts in order to build its theoretical constructs. A critical analysis of some of these major studies offers a general critique of the conflict and conflict management literature.

Because conflict and violence have been considered to be pathological, cross-national studies focusing on them represent one of the most highly developed areas of political inquiry. These studies have proliferated due to the ready availability of aggregate data on performance of individual countries and of "events data" for easy construction of indices of conflict and violence. These data sets have facilitated testing of hypotheses generated by theories often developed at other levels of analysis. Nonetheless, cross-national studies of conflict and violence are often disappointing because refined theory has not always guided data collection efforts, and the level of theoretical sophistication in conceptualization has been relatively low.

The most common method of *identifying* and *quantifying* violence within countries has been to count or count-and-scale the number of violent incidents reported in readily available sources of information. Rummel and Tanter, in an extensive cross-national study of conflict, have used simple reports of acts of violence as indicators.[1] Feierabend and Feierabend have created six and seven point severity of events scales made up of subjective judgments about the relative severity of various reported incidents.[2] Tilly and Rule have concentrated on "man days" of participation in disruption, which meant counting violent occurrences and estimating the size of crowds involved.[3] Gurr has attempted to synthesize these approaches by using measures of the *scope* of violent acts in terms of citizen participation, *intensity* or destructiveness of actions, and *duration* of violence.[4] He claims each of these aspects of violence to be analytically separable from the others. A country could be beset with conflict of great scope with millions of participants, but the intensity of violence might not be great. An example of this would be a prolonged general strike. Similarly, violence could involve destruction of great intensity, but would not necessarily mean that great numbers of people would be involved for a long duration.

These efforts to quantify overt violence cannot, however, measure two other very important aspects: the level of repressed violence and the propensity to do violence. Absence of reported conflict does not mean that a country is inhabited by peace-loving people. As Coser has pointed out, it may be a sign of hostility.[5] Use of force may well keep a highly dissatisfied populace from engaging in violence, although beneath the surface discontent may be quite widespread. Counting and quantifying events may yield some insight into conditions under which violence has occurred, but such an approach does not always lend itself to predicting where violence will break out in the future.

Efforts to measure conflict and violence cross-nationally have been paralleled by attempts *to make conceptual sense* out of the broad spectrum of known types of disturbances. Rummel, for example, has created a list of twenty-five types of domestic violence, a significant effort but one of value mainly to those persons highly specialized in esoteric aspects of conflict.[6] Eckstein has developed a more parsimonious typology suggesting unorganized spontaneous violence, intra-elite conflicts, two types of revolution, and wars of independence as headings under which political violence could be categorized.[7] In more commonly understood language, these types of violence would be called riots, coups d'etat, and various forms of revolution and wars of liberation. Rummel, Gurr, and others have used a mathematical technique called factor analysis to create groupings of violent acts empirically from existing data.

Gurr's factor analysis has yielded three "dimensions" of conflict within nation-states: turmoil, conspiracy, and internal war. Turmoil occurs most frequently and consists of "relatively spontaneous, unorganized political violence with substantial popular participation. . . ." This kind of violence includes strikes, riots, localized rebellions, and similar types of actions. Turmoil is characterized by lack of organization and planning and often can be triggered by a single event that unleashes a torrent of pent-up aggressions. The shooting of a young member of a minority group at the scene of a crime can trigger a riot in a tense minority community, or raising prices just before Christmas in a centralized economy can lead to strikes and riots as it did in Poland in late 1970 and early 1971.

Conspiracy is defined as "highly organized political violence with limited participation. . . ." Conspiracies are most familiar to those studying politics in developing nations. The essential features of conspiracy are tight organization and limited scale. Military takeovers are characterized by a tightly conspiratorial nature and a limited amount of bloodshed. In many cases of conspiracy one set of ruling political elites is simply replaced by another, and life changes very little for the common man. Conspiratorial upheavals are common in Latin America, where political instability, military governments, and dictatorships have become accepted ways of life.

Internal war is "highly organized political violence with widespread popular participation designed to overthrow a regime or dissolve a state. . . ."[8] It includes guerrilla warfare that becomes successful, civil wars such as those that tore apart Indochina for two decades, and large-scale ethnic conflicts that occur in those areas of the world involved in the process of "nation-building."

Hibbs has concentrated specifically on "mass political violence." He carefully defines mass political violence as conflict having an antisystem character, being of immediate political significance, and involving collective activity.[9] Hibbs finds six categories of events that could be called mass political violence: riots, armed attacks, political strikes, assassinations, death from political violence, and antigovernment demonstrations. He subjected his data to factor analysis to determine the underlying dimensions of mass political violence. He concludes that there are two dimensions of violence and labels them collective protest and internal war.

Gurr has created a three-fold *typology of theories of conflict:*

those of a social-psychological nature, social-structural theories, and group conflict theories.[10] Theory building to date has concentrated most heavily on social-psychological variables. Gurr has relied heavily on the concept "relative deprivation" to explain the psychological dynamics behind violence and aggression. Gurr makes a significant distinction between *instigating* and *mediating* variables that determine civil strife, and he concludes that those countries in which citizens feel deprived relative to some reference group are countries that are most likely to experience civil violence.[11] Davies originated the idea of a "J-curve" of rising expectations leading to change that precedes revolution. A long period of rising expectations and gratifications is often followed by a sharp reversal during which a gap between expectations and gratifications quickly widens.[12] Davies' ideas have been refined and incorporated in the work of Gurr and that of Feierabend, Feierabend, and Nesvold.[13]

Social-structural theories of violence are based on concepts such as "strain" and "dysfunction." Social-structural theorists pay little attention to psychological variables and their emphasis is on linking social structural strain with violence. Smelser has identified six sets of social determinants of violence.[14] Johnson has proposed a structural theory of revolutionary conflict based upon "disequilibrium" in social systems.[15] Whatever the external or internal causes of such disequilibrium, ruling political elites must face up to it or they risk loss of legitimacy.

Group conflict theories take as their basic premise that violence arises out of group struggles over valued resources and positions. The extent to which group conflict precipitates violence is determined by a number of factors. Dahrendorf has claimed that class conflict is pervasive in all industrial societies at all times, since it results from continuous differential allocations of authority tied to structural differentiation resulting from industrialization. According to Dahrendorf, the intensity of class conflict increases with increasing organization, when class and group conflicts are coincident rather than dissociated, and when the distribution of authority and the distribution of rewards are closely associated.[16]

Marx was one of the first to write about the class base of group conflict. Marx saw economic change as exacerbating class conflict. The means of production (factories, raw materials, finance capital, etc.) fall into fewer and fewer hands as a result of periodic depressions, and the working class becomes oppressed to the point of rising and seizing the means of production from the oppressors.

Galtung introduced "rank disequilibrium" resulting from division of labor and social stratification as a concept that explains conflict. The hierarchical position of an individual or group relative to others is important in determining aggressive behavior.[17] Rank disequilibrium occurs when individuals or groups attain an inconsistent profile of valued conditions. A person or group with great wealth, for example, but possessing little power or prestige, would be disequilibriated and would attempt to even out the profile. Whether violence results depends largely on cultural experience and the success or failure of nonviolent attempts to restore equilibrium.

There have been fewer attempts to build theory from the reverse perspective: *attempts to account for stability* rather than violence. Hurwitz has documented five approaches to defining and measuring stability.[18] The first is to simply define stability as *lack of violence*. As in the case of studies of violence, stable political systems have been defined through simple counting operations. Those countries with fewest reported violent events are defined as stable. Political stability is also often defined in terms of *government longevity*. The longer a government remains in power the more stable the system is taken to be. The problems with this approach are obvious. Such stability may well represent repression or a "calm before the storm." Hurwitz also lists *existence of a legitimate constitutional order, absence of structural change*, and a *residual "multifaceted" category* as other approaches to defining and measuring political stability.

All of these approaches have some utility in studying cross-national differences in levels of violence and stability. But each only captures part of the total picture. Too frequently easily available data has shaped the nature of conceptualization and set the limits of theory-building. More grandiose attempts to create a general theory of political violence through causal modeling, however, have often included such a wide variety of poorly measured variables that the findings have been impossible to comprehend and meaningless in terms of policy recommendations.[19] The real political world is terribly complex, but unneeded complexity has often been introduced through use of inadequate and inappropriate measures and the introduction of variables that would not be required if adequate theoretical constructs guided data collection.

Refining Concepts

Ironically, one of the major barriers to advancing our knowledge of conflict and conflict management in cross-national studies has been a lack of political sophistication in concept formation. Conflict theorists have borrowed heavily, and sometimes uncritically, from many other disciplines. Relative deprivation, alienation, frustration, aggression, territoriality, disequilibrium, strain, etc. are all terms that have been freely imported from other fields. These borrowed concepts are sometimes of dubious value. In a sense, their availability might well have retarded development of a more *political* science of conflict and conflict management.

Borrowing from other disciplines has not only retarded strictly political conceptualization, but has also led to *uncritical transference of findings* from one discipline to another. Frustration-aggression hypotheses, for example, were developed largely as a result of experimental studies of animals. But rats and pigeons operate at a much lower level of complexity than human beings. It is questionable, for example, if Calhoun's celebrated studies of crowding and aberrant behavior among rats are directly transferable to human beings who experience "subjective" feelings about crowding.[20] Similarly, Ardrey and others have expanded concepts such as territoriality from animal to human domains without thinking through differences that exist between supposedly rational human beings, and other animals.[21] Obviously, findings from other disciplines are important in building political theory, but political scientists should use caution in transferring hypotheses from other disciplines.

Another way in which the political study of conflict has lacked sophistication lies in ethnocentric and parochial definitions of conflict and violence.[22] While cross-national studies of conflict and violence represent the most important work done in this area, not enough attention has been paid to the *cross-cultural equivalence of concepts and measures*. Concepts and constructs in use have been anchored in industrial thought patterns and scholars have often been lax in asking critical questions about the applicability of measures to other cultures.[23] This indirectly raises the question about what should be measured in the first place. If concern is to be with the political *intent* of various actors, much more must be done to refine cross-cultural measures. It is often assumed, without any good reason, that assassinations, riots, national strikes, etc. have similar political meaning from one culture to another and that actors thus engaged have similar political intent. While arguing that these events do not have similar meanings for different actors in different cultures could be construed as an argument for research nihilism, if equivalent concepts cannot be found then the validity of the theory depending upon them must be called into question. The point to keep in mind is that much more care should be taken in creating and operationalizing complex constructs and measures to make certain that they adequately measure phenomena in the cultures to which they are to be applied.

In addition to validity questions, much more attention could be paid to broadening conceptual horizons and examining aspects of violence that have not yet received much scrutiny. Emphasis has been heavy on visible and easily counted outbreaks of antiestablishment violence in many theories, but there has been little similar recognition of repression, vigilante violence, and potential violence. Scholars have naturally followed the trail of available data and have rooted most theories in observable breakdowns of established political order.

Violence has also been defined narrowly as something done by unruly masses against established authorities and this has created a bias against rapid political change. There has been little analysis of *normative justifications* for violence. A revolt against an actively repressive political regime, perhaps in Uganda, Spain, or Czechoslovakia, scales the same as the actions of the Irish Republican Army against established authority in Ireland. While the violent acts may be similar in outward appearance, there are important moral distinctions that simply are not made in most studies utilizing aggregate data. In part, this has been due to a false sense of "objectivity" among political scientists; a feeling that there is something unscientific about making judgments based upon normative considerations. It is also much more time-consuming to deal with violence in a more sophisticated fashion, and conceptual richness has often been lost within computer programs.

Additional sophistication is also needed in differentiating violence of a political nature from more generalized violence. In many studies all violent incidents have been classified as political, or at least have been assumed to have some political meaning. Deaths from domestic violence, for example, have been very frequently used as an indicator of *political* instability and *political* pathology. Violent incidents not only carry different political meanings across cultures, they may have no political meaning at all. Tribal feuds, banditry, rape, assault, or labor violence need not be necessarily tied to or directed at political regimes; neither need suicide rates which, unfortunately, have often been taken as indicators of political pathology.

Existing terminology also lacks sophisticated approaches to *political conflict management*. There are two faces to the study of political conflict. One emphasizes violence and pathology, departure from norms, and has been much studied. The other face is the study of political stability; conditions under which conflict is minimized, ruling political elites perform optimally, and "just" or "good" societies are developed. It gives testimony to a fascination with pathology and lack of positive vision that research has ignored those conditions that develop consensus and enduring political stability.

The conceptual distinction between competition and conflict made by Mack and Snyder also suffers from lack of clarity. In many political cultures a distinction between conflict and competition cannot easily be made. In many countries the "understood" rules of the political game include the right to assassinate opponents. In the Soviet Union, for example, such rules have shifted from time to time, but there have been many periods in which forced labor, exile, or execution were accepted aspects of politics, at least among ruling political elites. Politics exists to channel, dampen, and routinize conflict, but there are political systems in which very rudimentary competition, i.e. conflict, still is considered within the rules. At the very least, additional dimensions must be added to the conflict-competition distinction if theorists are to continue to categorize political behavior in this manner.

Research dealing with *violence deliberately fostered by political regimes*, "vigilante" violence, has also been comparatively ignored. Rosenbaum and Sederberg have sketched out a framework for a theory of vigilantism, but much more attention could be paid to the use of force in defense of regimes, ideologies, etc.[24] Regimes perceived by citizens to be ineffective in maintaining a prevailing sociopolitical order are often "aided" by defendants of that order: violence in defense of "law and order." It is reasonable to expect that socioeconomic and political frustrations can be expressed both within and against established political regimes, and the circumstances in which different alternatives are chosen should certainly be studied further.

Finally, there are important questions about *parsimony of*

concepts and constructs that have been used to explain various types of violence. Gurr, Hibbs, and others have developed complex causal models to describe preconditions of political violence, often neglecting what Eckstein calls immediate precipitants.[25] Political issues and ideologies can be extremely important as both preconditions and precipitants of violence, but they do not fit easily into abstract models and therefore tend to be ignored.

The complexity of existing causal models derived from cross-national studies raises many questions about their utility. In the development of the science of astronomy, for example, attempts to retain a geocentric model of the universe led to development of incredibly complex models of planetary motion involving "epicycles," circular movements of bodies within already circular orbits. It is possible that the search for order in a somewhat suspect political data base has led to premature closure in theory building similar to the epicycle phenomenon. Perhaps causal relationships dealing with conflict are as complex as many scholars make them out to be. Perhaps attempts to develop a general theory of conflict are doomed to failure for this reason. But perhaps the wholesale importation of theories and concepts from other disciplines has needlessly complicated analysis. Parsimony is considered an essential criterion for the selection of good theories. But present theories of political violence are hardly parsimonious and they offer very few policy recommendations.

Methodological Questions

It is obvious that the methods by which data dealing with cross-national political conflict are collected greatly influence the theories that result. The data that are easiest to collect are aggregate data for individual countries. Subnational units, social groups, or even individuals are possible alternate units of analysis, but most of the past studies considered to be in the mainstream of conflict research have resulted from analysis of aggregate data. This type of data is often unreliable for many reasons.

Ruling political elites not only attempt to manage or suppress conflict, they also attempt to suppress *information about conflict.* Social unrest is not only embarrassing to regimes when information about it is circulated abroad, but such information can have a multiplier effect within the country in which unrest occurs. It is therefore in the interest of political leaders both to quell disturbances and to curtail information about them. This means, of course, that the data upon which many cross-national studies of conflict and violence have been based is at best shaky and at worst grossly distorted by differential reporting.

Even where outright political suppression of information is not a problem, there are other serious deficiencies in studies that rely on reports of violence in the press and similar sources. Data reported by "official" and "semiofficial" sources is likely to be tainted by selective reporting. In India in 1975, for example, foreign reporters were asked to sign pledges to submit stories to censorship or to leave the country. Many studies rely extensively upon simple frequency counts of various types of destabilizing events as reported in key newspapers. Anyone familiar with the international flow of communications would immediately suspect the objectivity of such reporting. News services can only cover a small number of potential trouble spots. Violence in many countries simply goes unnoticed because of lack of reporting. Quantitative estimates of numbers involved in such events also raise serious problems of perception. Reports are often made by "stringers," individuals paid by the story. Stringers not only have an interest in overestimating the magnitude of violence, but they may also have political beliefs that color their perceptions of events.

A related question inherent in cross-national studies using data generated by individual countries is the accuracy of statistics that are reported. Some countries are much more accurate in their reporting than others. In the United States, for example, the FBI has been accused regularly of juggling crime data for political purposes. The more carefully data are reported the higher the rate of crime appears to be and vice versa. Many countries only selectively report statistics on violence. Others do not report them at all. In the Soviet Union, for example, even natural disasters, plane accidents, and similar events are usually kept out of the news. A substantial number of countries, therefore, should be excluded from cross-national studies on the grounds that their data is more fabrication than fact. But exclusion of these countries would mean losing a fairly large number of the world's political units, and therefore researchers have been loathe to exclude them.

The use of aggregate data also tends to conceal intracountry differences. In many countries political violence has been confined to regions that historically have not been integrated with the rest of the country. It is questionable, for example, whether Italy or Austria should be declared politically unstable because of relatively localized violence that has occasionally taken place in the

Tyrol region. Similarly, should Greece or Turkey be assessed for the deaths that occurred on Cyprus? Are these deaths caused by domestic violence or should this be considered international warfare?

The tendency of research to follow available data has been exacerbated by "the law of the instrument." Briefly stated, the law dictates that the availability of new machines and techniques encourages scholarship to follow capacities, even when the data is neither sufficiently detailed nor accurate to warrant such treatment. The introduction of larger, high-speed computers, and new "canned" computer programs into political analysis has made sophisticated techniques available to those who often do not understand the processes involved. Detailed attention is paid to instrumentation and analysis while the rudimentary nature of the data and artifacts that may be included in it are ignored.

Some of the actual measures and constructs employed in theory-building in cross-national studies of violence offer specific examples of doubtful conceptual validity and reliability. Feierabend and Feierabend, for example, used a relationship between "want formation" and "want satisfaction" to explain systemic frustration leading to political violence.[26] As indicators of want formation they used literacy and urbanization. As indicators of want satisfaction they used per capita measures of calorie intake, gross national product, telephones, physicians, newspapers, and radios. It should be readily apparent that this line between want formation and want satisfaction is not very clear. Newspapers and radios could represent want formation as well as want satisfaction. Taking per capital calorie intake as an example, it is a very unreliable measure in many respects. Calories, per se, tell us very little about diets. A person could receive an adequate number of calories by eating only sugar, but that person would probably soon die. Furthermore, an adequate supply of protein is much more essential to human health than is a large number of calories. Then there is the question of inequality of calorie consumption within a population. If the very rich get most of the calories and the very poor get very few, people could be dying in the streets from hunger while the aggregate figures would show a reasonably high average level of calorie consumption. Finally, there is only the most tenuous of links between calories actually consumed and citizen perception of calories that should be consumed.

Each of the variables used to create these want satisfaction indices could be subjected to similar observations. Feierabend and

Feierabend should not be singled out for special criticism, however. Their work is typical of much theory-building using these types of data.

Gurr has based his theories of conflict and violence very heavily on the relative deprivation concept. His use of relative deprivation, however, leaves something to be desired. In one study, "persisting deprivation" was defined by measures of potential separatism, dependence on foreign capital, religious cleavages, and lack of educational opportunities, among others.[27] Again, the relationship between these measures and relative deprivation as subjectively experienced by individuals is obscure.

These and other studies offer examples of parochialism and ethnocentrism in theory-building. In the United States scholars associate increasing real wages, intergenerational mobility, occupational advancement, etc. with feelings of want satisfaction. But it cannot be assumed that similar indices of satisfaction can be applied to many different cultures. In some cultures, for example, working for profit is not an idea that is well understood. Neither are many other aspects of achievement that we tend to take for granted in western industrial societies. Given this problem, it is difficult to see the applicability of many of these generalized indices and constructs to violence in nonindustrial cultures.

Measuring violence is also full of difficulties. Normal practice in cross-national studies has been to label all overt signs of violent behavior as equally negative and serious events. But an incident that appears to carry the same meaning in different cultures may be perceived differently by the people involved. A national strike or a riot in India would certainly not carry the same meaning as a national strike or riot in the United States. In the former country such incidents have become an almost routine part of political competition. In the latter country the subjective significance of such a dramatic departure from normality would be much greater. Similarly, police truncheons are routinely used against unruly student demonstrators in Japan, but such use of force would be roundly condemned in the United States. These subjective distinctions, however, have been all but ignored in most of these studies.

Ruling political elites also have different standards of conflict tolerance. While it is customarily assumed that leaders strive to routinize conflict and to turn it into competition, this is not always the case. Leaders frequently foment strife between potentially powerful subgroups in political systems in order to keep them weak and thereby to promote the overall stability of the whole political system. Summary measures may uncritically include elite-exacerbated conflict as an indicator of system instability when in reality the conflict has been created to sustain the system. There are big differences among elite conflict management, conflict dampening, conflict exacerbation and conflict elimination that are not adequately reflected in existing studies.

On the other side of the coin, studies using democracy and stability as key concepts have also suffered from lack of explicit, useful, and inclusive measurement rules.[28] Repressive dictatorships, for example, have often scaled out to be extremely stable political systems because of failure to measure repressed and potential violence. This can result in supposedly stable dictatorships, such as Portugal in 1975, suddenly being overturned by revolutions. Measurement of complex, but poorly defined concepts such as democracy has also been loosely handled. There are many subtle dimensions of democracy that have been ignored, and countries offering individual citizens very different types of freedoms are often lumped together in the same category.[29]

There is also a need in future studies to map out the social-psychological linkage in conflict and violence more carefully.[30] Psychological theories have yielded worthwhile hypotheses about individual violent behavior and aggregate data has yielded some additional, though suspect, information about national violence. Much work remains to be done in between, linking individual discontent and frustration with the violence expressed in aggregate data. For now, the territory in between remains a black box. Scholars suspect some things about the mix of individual attitudes that become linked to aggregate outcomes, but they are much less familiar with the inner workings of the box: the structure and processes that convert individual and group attitudes into social movements and collective protest.

It is also imperative in future studies to begin to close the gap between *objective* quantification of violence and *subjective* experience of that violence. It is very strange, for example, that a book could be written about why men rebel without interviewing anyone in a state of rebellion. There are, of course, significant barriers to doing survey research among revolutionaries. More seriously, however, existing studies have frequently not been informed by a revolutionary perspective and could profit from more attention to subjective reports of perceived oppression and deprivation.

Some Conclusions

From this overview of political conflict literature as reflected in cross-national studies it is obvious that certain areas of research may be classified as "information intensive" and "knowledge shy." Simple production or analysis of information does not necessarily increase understanding. Many studies of conflict have capitalized on machine manipulation of aggregate data because both data and machines were readily available. The question "what kind of data do I need" has not always been carefully posed before research has been undertaken. Obviously there is a dilemma here. Attempting to create more refined concepts and measures could well lead to theories with no supporting data. But uninformed data manipulation can lead to inadequate and inaccurate theories.

It is also implicitly assumed that violence, rebellion, turmoil, etc., being very visible phenomena, are the aspects of conflict that are most worthy of attention. This leaves many important questions unanswered. Much more attention should be paid to the theoretical question of how authority and legitimacy are established in political systems over time. There is also a series of questions that could be asked about repressed violence, alienation, and potential political conflict. Largely because such concepts do not readily lend themselves to immediate quantification, attention has been focused in these other areas.

The role of ruling political elites in preserving political stability also requires much more attention. Some regimes are capable of inspiring citizen confidence while others fail miserably. A theory of competent leadership should certainly be part of the conflict literature. This is only part of a more general problem of lack of attention to *conflict management*. Much more is known about conditions that lead to the deterioration of political order than about conditions and actions that maintain order.

Finally, much more attention should be paid to the important link between technology, social change, and patterns of political authority. Too frequently theories of conflict fail to note adequately the changing nature of technological parameters. As the technological and social environments within which politics takes place change so do the *relevant variables* and even *causal relation-*

ships that are essential components of theories of conflict. The role of mass media in exacerbating or managing conflict, for example, has certainly been enhanced by technological developments. Similarly, many issues that used to excite political passions are often no longer found to be exciting. Today's young citizens find it difficult to get excited over issues of religious freedom, while their ancestors thought religious freedom to be an issue of the utmost importance. Too little attention has been paid to rates of change as a relatively static view of conflict dynamics has been predominant.

REFERENCES

1. R. Rummel, "Dimensions of Conflict Behavior Within and Among Nations," in *General Systems Yearbook VIII* (1963), and R. Tanter, "Dimensions of Conflict Behavior Within and Between Nations, 1958–1960," *Journal of Conflict Resolution* (March 1966).
2. I. Feierabend and R. Feierabend, "Aggressive Behavior Within Politics, 1948–1962: A Cross-National Study," *Journal of Conflict Resolution* (September, 1966).
3. C. Tilly and J. Rule, *Measuring Political Upheaval*. Princeton: Center of International Studies, Monograph #19, 1965.
4. T. Gurr, *Why Men Rebel*. Princeton: Princeton University Press, 1970, p. 9.
5. L. Coser, *The Functions of Social Conflicts*. Glencoe, Ill.: The Free Press, 1956, pp. 81–85.
6. Rummel, "Dimensions of Conflict Behavior Within and Among Nations."
7. H. Eckstein, "On the Etiology of Internal Wars," *History and Theory* (#2, 1965).
8. The preceding quotations are from Gurr, *Why Men Rebel*, p. 11.
9. D. Hibbs, *Mass Political Violence*. New York: Wiley, 1973, ch. 2.
10. T. Gurr, "The Revolution-Social Change Nexus: Some Old Theories and New Hypotheses," *Comparative Politics* (April 1973).
11. Gurr, *Why Men Rebel*, ch. 2.
12. J. Davies, "Toward a Theory of Revolution," *American Sociological Review* (February 1962).
13. I. Feierabend, R. Feierabend, B. Nesvold, "Social Change and Political Violence: Cross-National Patterns," in I. Feierabend, R. Feierabend, T. Gurr, eds., *Anger, Violence, and Politics: Theories and Research*. Englewood Cliffs, N.J.: Prentice-Hall, 1972.
14. N. Smelser, *Theory of Collective Behavior*. New York: Free Press, 1963, esp. pp. 15–18.

15. C. Johnson, *Revolutionary Change*. Boston: Little, Brown, 1966.
16. R. Dahrendorf, *Class and Class Conflict in Industrial Society*. Stanford: Stanford University Press, 1959.
17. J. Galtung, "A Structural Theory of Aggression," *Journal of Peace Research* (#2, 1964); and J. Galtung, "A Structural Theory of Imperialism," *Journal of Peace Research* (#8, 1971).
18. L. Hurwitz, "Contemporary Approaches to Political Stability," *Comparative Politics* (April 1973).
19. Hibbs, *Mass Political Violence*, offers one of the best examples. The constructs involved are often so far removed from everyday experience that policy-makers would have a difficult time finding any concrete policy recommendations in it.
20. J. Calhoun, "Population Density and Social Pathology," *Scientific American* (February 1962).
21. R. Ardrey, *The Territorial Imperative*. New York: Atheneum, 1966.
22. See W. Welsh, *Studying Politics*. New York: Praeger, 1973, pp. 222–23.
23. A good discussion of cross-cultural validity of concepts in use is found in A. Przeworski and H. Teune, *The Logic of Comparative Social Inquiry*. New York: Wiley, 1970.
24. H. Rosenbaum and P. Sederberg, "Vigilantism: An Analysis of Establishment Violence," *Comparative Politics* (July 1974).
25. T. Gurr, *Why Men Rebel*, ch. 10; D. Hibbs, *Mass Political Violence*, New York: Wiley, 1973; and H. Eckstein, "On the Etiology of Internal Wars," in Feierabend, Feierabend, Gurr, eds., *Anger, Violence, and Politics*, pp. 13–18.
26. I. Feierabend and R. Feierabend, "Systemic Conditions of Political Aggression: An Application of Frustration-Aggression Theory," in Feierabend, Feierabend, Gurr, eds., *Anger, Violence, and Politics*.
27. T. Gurr, "A Causal Model of Civil Strife: A Comparative Analysis Using New Indices," *The American Political Science Review* (December 1968).
28. See L. Hurwitz, "Contemporary Approaches to Political Stability," *Comparative Politics* (April 1973) for an analysis of the weaknesses of many cross-national studies of stability.
29. See, for example, the critique of studies of ecnomic development and democracy by D. Neubauer, "Some Conditions of Democracy," *American Political Science Review* (December 1967).
30. See, for example, H. Cantril, *The Psychology of Social Movements*. New York: Wiley, 1941.

SELECTED BIBLIOGRAPHY

ALMOND, G., AND G. POWELL. *Comparative Politics: A Developmental Approach.* Boston: Little, Brown, 1966.

AZRAEL, J. *Managerial Power and Soviet Politics.* Cambridge: Harvard University Press, 1966.

BACHRACH, P. *The Theory of Democratic Elitism: A Critique.* Boston: Little, Brown, 1967.

BECK, C., ed. *Comparative Communist Political Leadership.* New York: McKay, 1973.

BELL, D. *The Coming of Post-Industrial Society: A Venture in Social Forecasting.* New York: Basic Books, 1973.

BENDIX, R. *Nation-Building and Citizenship: Studies of Our Changing Social Order.* New York: Wiley, 1964.

BENTLY, A. *The Process of Government.* Evanston, Ill.: Principia Press, 1935.

BERKOWITZ, L. *Aggression: A Social Psychological Analysis.* New York: McGraw-Hill, 1962.

BINDER, L., ed. *Crises and Sequences in Political Development.* Princeton: Princeton University Press, 1971.

BORGSTROM, G. *Focal Points: A Global Food Strategy.* New York: Macmillan, 1973.

———. *The Hungry Planet: The Modern World at the Edge of Famine.* New York: Macmillan, 1965.

BRONFENBRENNER, U. *Two Worlds of Childhood.* New York: Pegasus, 1970.

BROWN, L. *By Bread Alone.* New York: Praeger, 1975.

BRZEZINSKI, Z. *Between Two Ages: America's Role in the Technetronic Era.* New York: Viking Press, 1970.

———. *Ideology and Power in the Soviet Union.* New York: Praeger, 1967.

CANTRIL, H. *The Psychology of Social Movements.* New York: Wiley, 1941.

CHOUCRI, N., AND R. NORTH. *Nations in Conflict: National Growth and International Violence.* San Francisco: W. H. Freeman, 1975.

CHOUCRI, N. *Population Dynamics and International Violence: Propositions, Insights, and Evidence.* Lexington, Mass.: Heath, 1974.

CLARK, JR., R. *Development and Instability: Political Change in the Non-Western World.* Hinsdale, Ill: Dryden Press, 1974.

CONQUEST, R. *The Great Terror: Stalin's Purge of the Thirties.* New York: Macmillan, 1968.

COSER, L. *The Functions of Social Conflict.* Glencoe, Ill.: Free Press, 1956.

DAHL, R. *After the Revolution?: Authority in a Good Society.* New Haven: Yale University Press, 1970.

———. *Polyarchy: Participation and Opposition.* New Haven: Yale University Press, 1971.

DAHRENDORF, R. *Class and Class Conflict in Industrial Society.* Stanford: Stanford University Press, 1959.

DALY, H., ed. *Toward a Steady-State Economy.* San Francisco: W. H. Freeman, 1973.

DE SCHWEINITZ, K. *Industrialization and Democracy.* New York: Free Press, 1963.

DEUTSCH, K. *Nationalism and Social Communication: An Inquiry into the Foundations of Nationality.* Cambridge: M.I.T. Press, 1953.

———. *The Nerves of Government.* New York: Free Press, 1963.

DJILAS, M. *The New Class.* New York: Praeger, 1954.

DOLLARD, J. *Frustration and Aggression.* New Haven: Yale University Press, 1939.

DOMHOFF, G. *Who Rules America?* Englewood Cliffs, N.J.: Prentice-Hall, 1967.

DOWNS, A. *An Economic Theory of Democracy.* New York: Harper and Row, 1957.

EHRLICH, P., A. EHRLICH, AND J. HOLDREN. *Human Ecology: Problems and Solutions.* San Francisco: W. H. Freeman, 1973.

ETZIONI, A. *A Comparative Analysis of Complex Organizations.* New York: Free Press, 1961.

FALK, R. *This Endangered Planet.* New York: Random House, 1971.

FEIERABEND, R., I. FEIERABEND, AND T. GURR, EDS. *Anger, Violence, and Politics: Theories and Research.* Englewood Cliffs, N.J.: Prentice-Hall, 1972.

FINLAY, D., O. HOLSTI, AND R. FAGEN. *Enemies in Politics.* Chicago: Rand McNally, 1967.

FREEDMAN, A., AND P. E. FREEMAN. *The Psychology of Political Control.* New York: St. Martin's Press, 1975.

GEERTZ, C., ed. *Old Societies and New States: The Quest for Modernity in Asia and Africa.* New York: Free Press, 1963.

GILISON, J. *British and Soviet Politics: Legitimacy and Convergence.* Baltimore: The Johns Hopkins University Press, 1972.

GOULET, DENIS. *The Cruel Choice.* New York: Atheneum, 1975.

GURR, T. *Why Men Rebel.* Princeton: Princeton University Press, 1970.

HIBBS, D. *Mass Political Violence.* New York: Wiley, 1973.

HOLLANDER, G. *Soviet Political Indoctrination: Developments in Mass Media and Propaganda since Stalin.* New York: Praeger, 1972.

Selected Bibliography

HOPKINS, M. *Mass Media in the Soviet Union.* New York: Pegasus, 1970.

HOUGH, J. *The Soviet Prefects: The Local Party Organs in Industrial Decision-Making.* Cambridge: Harvard University Press, 1969.

HUNTINGTON, S. *Political Order in Changing Societies.* New Haven: Yale University Press, 1968.

JOHNSON, C. *Revolutionary Change.* Boston: Little, Brown, 1966.

KASSOF, A. *The Soviet Youth Program.* Cambridge: Harvard University Press, 1965.

KELLER, S. *Beyond the Ruling Class: Strategic Elites in Modern Society.* New York: Random House, 1963.

KORNHAUSER, W. *The Politics of Mass Society.* New York: Free Press, 1959.

LERNER, D. *The Passing of Traditional Society: Modernizing the Middle East.* New York: Free Press, 1958.

LINDBLOM, C. *The Intelligence of Democracy: Decision-Making Through Mutual Adjustment.* New York: Free Press, 1965.

LIPSET, S. M. *Political Man: The Social Bases of Politics.* New York: Doubleday, 1960.

LORENZ, K. *On Aggression.* New York: Harcourt, Brace & World, 1966.

LOWI, T. *The End of Liberalism: Ideology, Policy and the Crisis of Public Authority.* New York: Norton, 1969.

MCCONNELL, G. *Private Power and American Democracy.* New York: Knopf, 1966.

MEADOWS, D. *The Limits to Growth.* New York: Universe Books, 1972.

MESAROVICH, M., AND E. PESTEL. *Mankind at the Turning Point.* New York: Dutton, 1974.

MICHELS, R. *Political Parties.* New York: Free Press, 1959.

MILLS, C. W. *The Power Elite.* New York: Oxford University Press, 1956.

MOORE, JR., B. *Social Origins of Dictatorship and Democracy.* Boston: Beacon Press, 1966.

PARK, CHARLES. *Earthbound: Minerals, Energy and Man's Future.* San Francisco: Freeman, Cooper, 1975.

PETTMAN, RALPH. *Human Behavior and World Politics.* New York: St. Martin's Press, 1975.

PIRAGES, D., AND P. EHRLICH. *Ark II: Social Response to Environmental Imperatives.* San Francisco: W. H. Freeman, 1974.

PIRAGES, D. *Modernization and Political-Tension Management: A Socialist Society in Perspective.* New York: Praeger, 1972.

PREWITT, K., and A. STONE. *The Ruling Elites: Elite Theory, Power and American Democracy.* New York: Harper and Row, 1973.

PRZEWORSKI, A., AND H. TEUNE. *The Logic of Comparative Social Inquiry.* New York: Wiley, 1970.

SAKHAROV, A. *Progress, Coexistence, and Intellectual Freedom.* New York: Norton, 1968.

SCHATTSCHNEIDER, E. *The Semi-Sovereign People: A Realist's View of Democracy*. New York: Holt, Rinehart & Winston, 1960.
SCOTT, J. *Comparative Political Corruption*. Englewood Cliffs, N.J.: Prentice-Hall, 1972.
SKILLING, G., AND F. GRIFFITHS. *Interest Groups in Soviet Politics*. Princeton: Princeton University Press, 1971.
SMELSER, N. *Theory of Collective Behavior*. New York: Free Press, 1963.
SPROUT, H., AND M. SPROUT. *Toward a Politics of the Planet Earth*. New York: Van Nostrand Reinhold, 1971.
STENT, G. *The Coming of the Golden Age: A View of the End of Progress*. Garden City, N.Y.: Natural History Press, 1969.
STORR, A. *Human Aggression*. New York: Atheneum, 1968.
TRUMAN, D. *The Governmental Process*. New York: Knopf, 1951.
VACCA, R. *The Coming Dark Age*. Garden City, N.Y.: Anchor Books, 1974.
WEINER, M., ed. *Modernization: The Dynamics of Growth*. New York: Basic Books, 1966.
WELCH, C., ed. *Political Modernization*. Belmont, Calif.: Wadsworth, 1967.

INDEX

access, 23, 71, 94–95
achievement, recruitment by, 22
Almond, G., 13, 28
Ardrey, R., 129
ascription, recruitment by, 22
aspirational deprivation, 63
authority, 17, 34, 61

Bachrach, P., 81
Banks, A., 23, 71
Baratz, M., 81
behavioral sink, 3
Bell, D., 117–18
Bolsheviks, 92
Bronfenbrenner, U., 102
Brzezinski, Z., 111

Calhoun, J., 3, 129
censorship, 103, 132–33
Clark, R., 48
coercion, 33
cognitive dissonance, 57
competence, 30
competition, defined, 6
compliance, 31–36
conflict, defined, 6
conflict displacement, 15
conflict management, defined, 13
consensus, 81–84, 102, 104, 122
consensus of intensities, 81
consensus of views, 81

conspiracy, 126
convergence, 111
cooperation, 13
Coser, L., 16, 125
covariance, 11
criteria for authority, 30
cross-cutting cleavages, 74
cross-pressures, 74
crowding, 3
Cutright, P., 42

Dahl, R., 30, 71
Dahrendorf, R., 127
Davies, J., 127
death instinct, 4
decremental deprivation, 63
democracy, as conflict management, 70–76, 122
democratic centralism, 93
De Schweinitz, K., 55, 65
Deutsch, K., 11, 36, 47
dictatorship of the proletariat, 92
diffusion, of ideas, 58
disequilibrium, 127
Djilas, M., 111
Doob, L., 48
Downs, A., 81

Easton, D., 14
Eckstein, H., 28, 58, 125, 132
economic conflict, 7

145

economics of scale, 47
economy, criterion of, 30
elections, 72, 77, 87
elections, Soviet, 98–100
empathy, 48
environment, physical, 115, 118–121
environment, social, 115
ethnicity, 10
Etzioni, A., 33

Federal Trade Commission, 79
Feierabend, I., 124, 127, 134
Feierabend, R., 124, 127, 134
food, 119–120
fossil fuel subsidy, 119
Freud, S., 4
Fromm, E., 4
frustration, 4

Galtung, J., 128
gatekeepers, 104
Gilison, J., 17
Glavlit, 103
green revolution, 120
Gregg, R., 23, 71
Gurr, T., 63, 125, 126, 127, 132, 135

heterophily, 58
Hibbs, D., 126, 132
hierarchical decision-making, 93
Hobbes, T., 2
homophily, 58
human needs, 9
Huntington, S., 61, 65
Hurwitz, L, 128

ideology, 11, 110–111
industrialization, 40, 47, 50, 119
industrialization, socialist, 110
information management, 37

inhibitory mechanisms, 2
Inkeles, A., 48
insulation of elites, 24
internal war, 126
iron law of oligarchy, 21

Kahl, J., 48
Kassof, A., 102
Keller, S., 86
Khrushchev, N., 97
Komsomol, 101
Kornhauser, W., 74

Lasswell, H., 32
law of the instrument, 134
legitimacy, defined, 17
Lenin, V., 92
Lerner, D., 48
letters to the editor, 106
Liberman Plan, 107
limited government, 24, 82
limits to growth, 119, 120
Lindblom, C., 74
Line of Business Reporting Program, 79
Lipset, S., 41, 73
lobbying, 77
Lorenz, K., 2
Lowi, T., 85

Mack, R., 6, 131
Marshall, T., 53
Marx, K., 8, 93, 127
Maslow, A., 9
mass media, 103–106
Michels, R., 21
middle class, 64
Milgram, S., 4
military, in politics, 109
Mills, C., 86
minerals, 120
modernization, 47–49

Index

Monkey Wrench Syndrome, 122
Moore, B., 54
myths of democracy, 72–76

National Environmental Protection Act, 83
nationalism, 11
nation-building, 52
natural selection, 2
neo-colonialism, 60
Nesvold, B., 127
Neubauer, D., 43
new-class, 107–108, 111
nondecision, 81
nuclear power, 122

obedience to authority, 4
Octoberists, 101
oligarchy, 21
oligopoly, 85
OPEC, 121

Parsons, T., 13
partisan mutual adjustment, 74
Perlmutter, A., 61
personal choice, 30
persuasion, 36
pervasiveness of control, 24
pioneers, 101
pluralism, 73
political apathy, 28
political decay, 66
political development, 41–44, 65
political efficacy, 48
political indoctrination, 100
political participation, 52
political socialization, 38, 101
political stability, 28, 131
pollution, 120
polyarchy, 71
Popovic, N., 111

position scarcity, 6
post-industrial society, 116–118
potential conflict, 12
potential issues, 81
potential political violence, 96
potlatch, 7
power elite, 86
Praetorian politics, 61
progressive deprivation, 63
psychic needs, 9
psychological distance, 5

quiet veto, 107

race, 10
rank disequilibrium, 128
regionalism, 10
regulatory agencies, 78
relative deprivative, 57, 63, 127, 135
religion, 11
remuneration, 33
resource scarcity, defined, 6
revolution of rising expectations, 8, 63
Riggs, F., 57
Rogers, E., 58
Roos, B., 3
Rosenbaum, H., 131
rotation rules, 100
Rule, J., 125
ruling elites, defined, 18, 22
ruling political elites, defined, 18, 22
Rummel, R., 124, 125
rumor, 104

Schattschneider, E., 15, 74
scope, of political control, 82
scope of control, 24–26
Scott, J., 61

Sederberg, P., 131
sham political competition, 98
Shoemaker, F., 58
silent majorities, 73
Simmel, G., 16
Skilling, G., 106
Smelser, N., 127
Snyder, R., 6, 131
social mobilization, 47
social paradigm, 7
Soviet interest groups, 106–110
Spiro, H., 81
stability, 128
Stalin, J., 92
state building, 51
state of nature, 2
Steady-State, 116
Storr, A., 4
Stouffer, S., 73
strategic elites, 86

Tanter, R., 124
territoriality, 2, 3
Tilly, C., 125
Truman, D., 86
turmoil, 126

unemployment, 64

Verba, S., 28

Wallich, H., 121
want formation, 134
want satisfaction, 134
water, 120
welfare, 52
Worker's Council, 109

youth groups, 101

Zaninovich, G., 109

The Author

DENNIS C. PIRAGES is Associate Professor of Government and Politics and Director of the Program in Technology, Resources, and Sustainable Growth at the University of Maryland, College Park. He is the author of *Modernization and Political Tension Management* and co-author of *Ark II: Social Response to Environmental Imperatives*. Professor Pirages received his doctorate from Stanford University. He is currently working on two books, one dealing with global resource problems and the other with the question of long-term sustainable growth.